Leadership for a New World

Leadership for a New World
The Organic Approach to Employee Engagement

Yvonne Thompson

CHSC, CHRP, MAL (Leadership)

CHANGE
Innovators Inc.

Leadership for a New World:
The Organic Approach to Employee Engagement
copyright © Yvonne Thompson 2010
Change Innovators Inc.
1317A Portage Avenue
Winnipeg, Manitoba
R3G 0V3
Canada
www.changeinnovators.com

Editor: Amanda Le Rougetel
Printed and bound in Canada by Friesens.
First printing

Library and Archives Canada Cataloguing in Publication

Thompson, Yvonne, 1960–
        Leadership for a new world : the organic approach to employee engagement / Yvonne Thompson.
Includes bibliographical references.
ISBN 978-0-9865893-0-0
1.   Leadership. 2. Management. 3. Organizational

effectiveness. 4. Teams in the workplace. I. Title.
HD57.7.T46 2010   658.4'092   C2010-902336-6

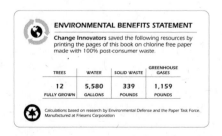

This work is dedicated to all of the managers, supervisors and leaders who are trying to find a holistic way to meet their employees' needs while increasing capacity, productivity and employee engagement.

Contents

Preface
Change is needed. Change is coming

My philosophy of New World Leadership has evolved organically through a series of events in my life and in collaboration with the team of great people I work with today. As the oldest member of our team (I recently turned 50), I find myself surrounded by members of Generation Y: 20-somethings who have a strong work ethic, clear goals, confirmed passions and significant talent. They bring a lot to their work in my business, Change Innovators Inc.—far more than anything I imagined they would when I opened my doors and hired my first employee in 2002.

When I hear business leaders complaining about "the younger generation" and their work ethic, I want to interject and debate with them. Yes, our younger employees have a different set of values than we (Baby Boomers) have, but that makes them just that—different, not wrong. They have clear expectations about work, work hours and work/life balance. At work, they want to contribute in a way that is meaningful to them, whatever that may mean to each individual.

I applaud them for being clear about what they want and what they expect from management. I believe that, in the right environment, younger employees will amaze us with their commitment, loyalty and accomplishments. They want to share, to contribute, to be part of a meaningful enterprise. But that "right environment" doesn't exist automatically. It must be consciously nurtured by leaders who genuinely want to <u>*work*</u> with their employees and who want to be New World Leaders.

The good news is that, as we head into the 21st century's second decade, I can feel change coming in the business community. I believe that everyone is eager for change in how we <u>*do*</u> our work and in how <u>*we*</u> are in business.

As a leadership consultant, I see more and more organizations developing leadership training initiatives, and it gives me hope that we are moving far beyond the limits of management training of the 1970s, 80s and 90s: We do not need any more courses on time management, supervising others, budgeting and negotiations. Numerous such courses already exist, offered by a variety of companies, educational institutions, consultants and trainers. Of course, the technical aspects of being a manager are important, but the true need in today's organizations is for authentic and conscious connections between individuals, within environments that encourage every person to be their very best, every day.

Recently, while teaching a Human Behaviour in Organizations course, I asked a group of managers if they had ever known a manager who was technically not very competent but who was, nonetheless, successful. From the back of the room, Sandra replied: "Yes. I worked for a manager who was an amazing success, one of the best managers in the organization. She was technically not very good but her ability to connect to the team and to create a team of high performers was amazing. We all loved working for her. It was one of the best jobs I ever had." I then asked Sandra how the manager could be successful if she was not technically proficient. It didn't take her long to reply: "We were all very willing to pick up the slack. In fact, we never talked about it. We loved working for her so much. It was just something we all did. It was not a big deal."

Sandra's comments reflect a common theme I hear in my work with clients, students and research participants: Employees are willing to commit themselves beyond the requirements of their job if—when—their manager engages them in genuine and meaningful ways.

Difficult People

Two years ago, I received a call from Jennifer, a potential client, who asked me if I would design and deliver a course for her organization on how to deal with difficult people. It took me just a moment to determine my response: "Have you considered why you have difficult people? How many people are you talking about?" Jennifer replied that they had a significant number of employees who were very difficult to deal with and she wanted someone to help the managers in dealing with them. I quietly advised that by looking at the "difficult people", she was looking at a symptom—not the cause—of the real problem and she would be wasting everyone's time. She was a little shocked, but didn't hang up. We talked some more.

What I discovered was that the group had been through a significant merger and buy-out. Silos existed throughout the organization; managers did not support each other but instead blamed each other for process problems and manufacturing deficiencies. Managers were telling their teams, "Stick with me and I will protect you." Each team worked in isolation from the others and did not see their impact on the larger unit. Solutions proposed in one area worked for that one area, but any resulting problems were always someone else's fault. It was a culture of blaming and finger pointing. Employees were unhappy and managers were uncooperative with each other. The organization's leaders took a strong command-and-control approach: It's our way or the highway, they implied. Managers were rarely consulted but always expected to execute the leadership's directives.

I'm happy to say that I did not develop and deliver a workshop on how to deal with difficult people. Instead, I worked with Jennifer to determine the real issues, separating out the symptoms and getting down to the root of the problem. Unfortunately, and as it goes with many initiatives, the process did not go as far as we would have liked it to. Fear got in the way: fear of letting go. Senior management was not ready to genuinely engage the managers in changing the organizational culture. It was just too big a leap for them.

New World Leadership

I believe it's time that organizational leaders take a long hard look in the mirror and consider these questions: Why should anyone want to come to work for this organization? What are we all about? What is great about becoming part of our team? These are hard questions that need meaningful answers. "Because we give them a paycheque" is no longer an adequate response! To remain competitive, to attract the best talent, to build effective employee engagement, organizations must change. Survival in the 21st century's business world, which is more holistic than mechanistic, more knowledge driven than task driven, more spiritually fed than ever before, organizations must change how they work. Same old same old is, quite simply, a recipe for failure.

New World Leadership at its roots is quite simple: Organizations must have a compelling purpose that matters. They must provide more than just a place to work. They must connect employees to something bigger than the bottom line. Leaders must be open and transparent: Use conscious dialogue. Expect the best of everyone. Build authentic relationships. Provide an environment where responsible self-management can flourish.

Simple, right? But if it's so simple, why don't more organizations use New World Leadership as their focus and business model? I suspect that there are many leaders who are not ready to give up their control and their power—of their organization or over "their" people. The few at the top like their position, their title and the authority granted them in the old mechanistic business model. However, I believe that, as the power continues to shift from the *employer* to the *employee* in today's labour-shortage knowledge-based economy, organizations of every size in every industry will need to adopt New World Leadership just simply to remain competitive. The old mechanistic approach won't work for them, because people won't work for those who use command-and-control management approaches.

People everywhere are yearning for a better place—a better way—to work than was available to their parents and grandparents. They want to contribute and feel valued in a genuine, meaningful and authentic way. They care about the planet, their environment and the lighter side of life. They are spiritual in a way that is unique to this newest group entering the workforce. They expect balance and sincerity grounded in real-life experiences. These younger workers are ready for New World Leadership. Are you ready to live it?

Thanks

I could never have written this book without the influence and inspiration of faculty members in the Master's in Leadership program at Royal Roads University in Victoria, B.C. They challenged my thinking and made me reflect on my assumptions, my beliefs and my philosophy. Thank you Niels Agger-Gupta, Maggi Feehan, Marilyn Hamilton and Marilyn Taylor. Also a very special thank you to Marie Graf, my academic supervisor, who was truly in my corner, believed in my work and never let me doubt myself.

My co-workers at Change Innovators Inc. are truly my second family. For their support, honesty and consistent desire to be their best and to make us all be our best, I am eternally grateful. Thank you Cory Graham, Shannon Graham, Don Gregory, James Irwin, Brian Roach, Mike Thompson and Jenn Trann.

My dear friends believed in me and supported me through this wild ride from idea to book. Amanda Le Rougetel, Shannon Martin, Irene Friesen-Hughes and Heather Racano: You gave me feedback on my writing and you supported my desire to introduce this New World Leadership to the business community. Thank you from the warmest place in my heart.

Note on Names

To protect privacy and ensure confidentiality, I have changed the names of individuals in this book, except for one who requested that I use his real name.

Leadership for a New World

Systems Thinking and Change

Shared Leadership

Authentic Relationships

Conscious and Intentional

Compelling Purpose

Values

Personal Development

Responsible Self-Management

Connection to Community

Chapter One

Introduction

My journey in business has taken me from the school of hard knocks to the world of holistic leadership.

Along the way, I have witnessed the stubbornness of human beings, the resiliency of individuals faced with difficult professional challenges, and the joy of connecting—really connecting—with people willing to learn new ways of working and leading.

In this chapter, I share the New World Leadership model and outline its capacity to transform how we do business in order to achieve heightened commitment, engagement and loyalty from stakeholders.

My Story

I was 38 years old when I was offered what I believed to be the career opportunity of a lifetime. During the previous 20 years, I had worked in the transportation industry in various capacities. I slowly had moved into management roles and was finding great interest in leading others. But this new opportunity was what I had been waiting for. It was 1998 and there were very few women running large transportation operations. I felt privileged to get this opportunity.

With my many years in the transportation sector, I was used to being the only female in a traditionally male industry. This did not concern me because now I would be the branch manager with significant autonomy and flexibility. I couldn't wait to get started.

Two business days prior to starting my new role, the departing manager asked me out for dinner. He was preparing to leave the city and move back home to take up a new position there. It was the Thursday evening prior to my start date on Monday morning. There would be no orientation or easing in period. He would leave for Calgary on Friday afternoon and I would start Monday morning. I was so excited.

During our dinner I could sense that Paul wanted to tell me something. We had a very nice meal and lots of small talk about the company and what I could expect corporately. Towards the end of the meal Paul quietly said, "You are going to hate it. This place is the most dysfunctional, angry and upsetting place to work. The employees hate the management and the management hate the employees. They are truly at war." I could not believe what he just said. But looking at him through my lovely rose-coloured glasses I simply said, "That is not possible. There is no way it could be that bad."

I would learn just how wrong I was.

The local branch had 225 employees (only four of them women), three managers, four lead hands and a sales team of four. All 225 employees were unionized through the same union and local, and we had two shop stewards. I genuinely believed there was no way a group of people could be as bad as Paul had described. It just wasn't possible. I had worked my entire 20-year career on the operations side of this industry and I had seen and experienced a lot, but never imagined what I was about to learn.

My introduction to the culture began slowly. My first walk through the warehouse required me to step over large gobs of spit mixed with sunflower seed shells. I was, to say the least, a little shocked. There was a sense of uneasiness about the place, but I did not let it bother me. I was determined to be a great manager—it was only a matter of time before I would have this place looking great. Call me naive.

As the first few weeks went by, I experienced a few comments that I thought were a bit inappropriate, but I didn't respond. For example, as I walked down the hall someone would quietly say, just within ear shot, "You'll never make it past 12 months." Or I might hear, "You are like all the rest. This should be fun."

It is helpful at this time to provide a little more context. I had worked within a unionized environment before, but I had never been the primary contact for ensuring a collective agreement was followed properly. I had handled many stage 1 grievances and a few at stage 2, but never before had I been the manager who would determine stage 2 and 3, along with the arbitration process. In my previous experiences as an operations manager, I had always had an HR department available to handle the difficult and escalated grievances. But this organization had a very small HR component and what was available was extremely limited and two provinces away. Many of the day-to-day decisions were made locally. By the branch manager. Me.

One Friday, close to the completion of my second month, I received 36 stage 2 grievances all on the same day. The rumour on the warehouse floor was that if they could find four more grievances and make it a nice round 40 in total, they could make me cry. Well. I couldn't tell anyone that I had been crying in my office since 10:30 that morning.

This was my new reality: Open Warfare. Employees did whatever they could to sabotage the efforts of management, and the managers and supervisors did what they could to sabotage the efforts of the union. It was a crazy place and I was in the middle of it.

In week 10, a chair was thrown at my office door by an employee who had been in a long and hard grievance with the previous manager and who wanted me to know just exactly how upset he was. There were many examples of extremely upset and angry people. I was in shock and disappointed by my situation, but I was also intrigued.

I kept asking myself, "How does a group of 225 employees become so angry and untrusting that they would collectively behave like this?" I had never experienced anything like it. The 80/20 rule wasn't applying at all: Work with the 80% of employees who want to do a good job and don't spend too much time trying to please the 20% who are really disgruntled. We had at least 95% of the unionized employees in complete anger and outrage most of the time, while the remaining 5% were not yet completely cynical.

By week 11, I had made two commitments to myself: First, try to understand what could have happened to make so many people so angry and hurt and disillusioned. Second, create a place from which to build trust and that would make people want to come to work again. These commitments put me on the journey of a lifetime. It wasn't easy, but it was rewarding.

It didn't take me long to figure out the answers to my first question: What happened to make so many people so unhappy? These employees had had four branch managers in six years, no consistency in approach or strategy, no clear direction. The culture at this branch was the culture the employees decided to create themselves, because they were the only consistent factor present. Rules were never consistently applied by the branch managers and, with little or no support from head office, they were left to manage however they wanted to. Some enjoyed meeting staff at the bar on Friday night. Others were strict disciplinarians. Still others were just not present; they would take extended time off golfing and doing whatever they felt like. I sensed that there had been little commitment to the people who did the actual work. Managers had not tried to connect with the employees as human beings, as real people who were just like them—just trying to feel they had made some progress by the end of each day.

My second commitment was to begin to build relationships, to find any way I could to make a connection with the human beings who worked in this building, many of whom had committed a significant portion of their lives to the organization. I started by delivering coffee.

Every Friday morning I would come in early and make large urns of coffee. I would put the urns on a trolley and go from overhead door to overhead door delivering coffee to the drivers. At first, they would not take the coffee, nor would they acknowledge me. I am not exaggerating; this is how bad it was. But after several weeks, slowly but surely they would take the coffee and say thanks. They wouldn't talk to me at first, but then gradually they would bring up work issues. It was more like complaining, but I was happy we were making a connection, even if it was simply to complain about something.

I tried really hard to get the staff to attend a meeting. This was next to impossible, so I decided that they needed an enticement. Am I the only manager who has driven through a McDonalds restaurant drive-thru window at 5:30am to order

$350 worth of Egg McMuffins? Well, that is what I did once a month. In the beginning, the staff would leave the warehouse when they could smell the hot food, grab a sandwich and head right back into the warehouse. But slowly, ever so slowly, they began to hang back to hear what I had to say. Over 18 months, I watched a group of people slowly warm up and come to life. I began to see a small glimmer of hope that maybe we could build relationships enough to make some progress. My goal was to be fair and consistent, always consistent. I wanted them to know that I wasn't going anywhere, that I would always have time to hear what they had to say. I had to build even just a small amount of trust before anyone would consider anything that I had to say.

I remember one of our most disgruntled employees. He was always openly negative and vocal about how much he hated the place, but one day I saw progress. I had overheard one of the other employees mention that Sam and his wife had just had their first baby a few days earlier. I immediately went out, bought a card and wrote simple heartfelt congratulations, and I intentionally mailed the card to his home, through the postal service. His wife, at home with their new little one, received the card. The following week, Sam came into my office and said, "Thank you. I had no idea you even knew, and no one here has ever done anything like that for me and my wife." Imagine that; a simple human-to-human experience, which should have been so normal for people who worked together, was considered a rarity.

I made a conscious effort to work with the managers to ensure that they understood the importance of connecting with this large group of people, without whom we would not be able to deliver our services. We met weekly and spoke about the grievances, the real issues and the efforts it would take to connect with the employees. As we entered our second year together, we began to see grievances go down, communication go up and gain a sense that maybe, just maybe, we could make a difference to this place. I started to believe that we could create a place where the team would actually enjoy coming to work. We had barbeques, celebrated birthdays and, more importantly, began to include the employees in decision-making and changes throughout the operation. They were thrilled to finally be asked for their opinions. Heading into the third year, we had only three grievances and what I would consider a respectful and certainly much more considerate workforce that included managers, supervisors and frontline contributors all bringing value to the organization.

None of this came easily. In my early days there, I lost many nights' sleep thinking about the issues, including the pressure from head office to improve efficiencies and the deep personal issues facing this team. I couldn't even begin to think about improving efficiency; I was still trying to get people to just talk to each other.

But the roots of change grow strong, if you nurture them. I am proud to say that many years later, one of the shop stewards who had been a true adversary of mine and made life very difficult for me in the early months was now seen as one of my teachers. I came to appreciate Randy's smart intellect and his tenacity and drive to win improvements for his union brothers. But it took me almost 3 years to appreciate that talent. He challenged me every day and made me stop and think about each decision. We kept each other honest and, over the years, built a relationship that was cooperative and consistent in approach.

He tracked me down almost seven years after I had left the position and asked me to be a reference for him as he changed careers. I felt privileged to do this for him. I remember standing in my new offices—the first office of Change Innovators Inc., and speaking to him about our time together at the transportation company. He thanked me for everything I had taught him and I was thrilled to tell him that the feeling was mutual.

My experience with this company was the beginning of my strong interest in human behaviour in organizations and human behaviour in general: What do people inherently want out of their time at work? What makes one person love getting up and contributing to their work, while another has trouble getting out of bed? I wanted to understand, so I decided to return to school and begin a new career, forge a new direction for myself.

I had been working in organizations for 20 years (1980 to 2000), and I was tired of seeing companies say one thing and do something completely different. I felt that they could articulate a vision when they wanted to connect to the team, but they weren't interested in executing on that vision. I have spent a significant amount of time trying to understand why senior leaders hold on to power and control. I wonder why they don't realize the huge advantage they gain when they give away the power and control and engage and connect with the entire organization through a belief that people generally want to do good and contribute their talents and skills.

One of my favourite quotes comes from the authentic and real leader Herb Kelleher, CEO of Southwest Airlines for many years. In a well known SWA video called "It's So Simple", when asked about how he keeps control of the many locations and

32,000 employees, he says, "Never had control. Never wanted control … The word power should only be used with speed boats and weightlifters." This is a true New World Leader. He recognized early on how important it is to engage your entire workforce in the objectives of the organization through inclusion and a humanistic, holistic and altruistic approach. It would appear that for Herb Kelleher, it was always about the people and the human side of business. When you make your number one customer your employees, how can you go wrong? Your employees will take care of the customer if you take care of the employees.

What is Your Story?

Have you ever had to work with (or live with) someone who preferred a command-and-control perspective or mechanistic style of leadership? Someone who preferred to make decisions independently with no input from others? A person who needed things to be done their way? Maybe it was a supervisor or manager, or maybe even a family member? How did you feel at that time? When you had a mechanistic leader, what was the work environment like? Were you highly productive and engaged in your work? Were you creative and innovative in problem solving? Did you feel comfortable taking your ideas and your suggestions forward? Or did you feel something completely different?

My Philosophy: New World Leadership

It is sometimes important to see clearly where we have been, so that we can begin to see clearly where we are going. When

I use the term *mechanistic*, I am referring to the management style of hard knocks, the "my way or the highway" approach to decision-making. If you can believe it, I spoke with someone just last year, who had a new boss arrive in the department and, in one of their first meetings, said to this long-term employee: "Fit in or eff off." Old fashioned as it may be, the mechanistic, command-and-control theory of management is still alive and well. But I believe there is hope.

Our new generations are changing the world. They are standing up and saying, "No more! We want to be included. We want to be heard. We want to contribute in a real and authentic way." This book is about the journey of leadership, about moving business management from mechanistic to holistic. It's a matter of survival. Society no longer accepts the command-and-control approach to business life, but instead believes that everyone should have the opportunity to contribute and must be appreciated for the role they play in their organization.

It used to be that leaders were focused solely on delivering results. Today, results remain important, but the focus includes delivering those results with humility, credibility and authenticity. People are looking for a different kind of leadership and in Chapters Two through Nine, I explore leadership through a new lens. I present New World Leadership as a holistic approach, and present a model that identifies the nine components of New World Leadership.

My New World Leadership model represents many of the understandings that I have developed over the last 10 years through my own research and discussions with front-line employees. I've had the opportunity to talk to people who've been in the workforce for only three or four years. Many of them are entering the most exciting times of their career. Some of them are as young as 25, others are coming into the peak of their career in their mid- to late 40s.

The New World Leadership model reflects the key components that 21st century employees are looking for—and it's not the old mechanistic style that has been so ingrained in our corporate world over the past 70 years. This is not only refreshing but exciting. Everyone I spoke to wants to contribute, wants to bring value to their organizations. They understand the importance of profitability and sustainability, but they want to shed the mechanistic, command-and-control approach. They want to help create organizations, led by New World Leaders who take a humanistic and holistic approach to business.

I invite you to read on … to journey into the world of New World Leadership.

Chapter Two

Compelling Purpose

Compelling
Purpose

KNOW YOUR COMPELLING PURPOSE

An organization's compelling purpose is deeply rooted in everything the organization does. It is a purpose that is felt to be of higher importance than profits and productivity alone. It drives and impacts decisions and actions throughout the organization. It is at the core of everything the company does.

Today, people have high expectations: They are seeking a more enriched, balanced and holistic approach to life and work. As a business owner or leader, you will need to be able to answer the questions: Why should someone work for you? Why should they engage their time, talent and effort in your company? What's in it for your employees beyond a pay-cheque? Your organization's compelling purpose will inform your answers.

The New World Leadership model requires you to make a significant paradigm shift. At the centre of this model is a compelling purpose, which takes us away from the mechanistic, industrial approach of leadership towards an all-encompassing humanistic approach to business and business success. An organization's compelling purpose is deeply rooted in everything the organization does. It is a purpose that is felt to be of higher importance than profits and productivity alone. It drives and impacts decisions and actions throughout the organization. It is at the core of everything the company does.

New World Leadership is about living out a true purpose that engages the individuals who work in the organization, as well as the larger community within which that organization operates. Companies can do this by showing and sharing their unique talent. Each organization is unique, just as each person who works and contributes to the organization is unique. The key is to find your unique purpose, to expose it and then to live it. At its most genuine, your compelling purpose doesn't fade and doesn't lose relevance or focus, even when times are tough.

Whether the organization's compelling purpose is grounded in the original founder's vision and emulated by the stakeholders or whether it is developed over time by the corporate culture and the internal stakeholders, a compelling purpose is at the root of all successful New World organizations. People will engage in a higher purpose and build an emotional connection to organizations that are rooted in an important cause beyond bottom-line profits. The compelling purpose does not have to change the world; it must simply impact the immediate community in some (even small) way. Some organizations and individuals are destined to live a compelling purpose of significant proportion, while others leave a tiny legacy that impacts only a few. Both paths are uniquely significant in their own way.

People of all ages are looking to work for an organization that has deeper meaning and broader objectives than strictly shareholder returns. They want to work for a company that has a larger, more significant impact on the community. So it's important for companies to look at why they are in business and why people should work for them. What's in it for employees beyond a paycheque? What does the company have or do that creates a connection with employees? When you consider the common needs of all human beings—the need to belong, to find meaning, to contribute, to have a level of personal control and to be valued for their contribution, it is no wonder people are looking to connect and engage with organizations that have a compelling purpose that resonates with them.

My research and work in the field of human behavior and organizational culture leads me to believe that it is not only young workers who are reaching out and asking businesses to be more than just a place to work, but many older workers are also beginning to look for this. Employees are willing to become fully engaged with their employer as long as there is accountability to something beyond bottom-line results and customer satisfaction. And let's face it. It can't all be about the customer. Organizations that focus strictly on customer satisfaction and believe that every dollar must be spent as close to the customer as possible risk losing the commitment and loyalty of their employees. This is simple human nature. Organizations often ask their employees to focus 100% of their efforts on efficiencies and customer service, but this can leave the employee asking, "What about me?" They are often not included, not consulted and left feeling unappreciated and underutilized.

Is it possible that a common thread running throughout all human beings is a need and desire to contribute in a bigger way? Research published in 1999 by the Gallup Group[1] suggested

---

1. as outlined in *First Break All the Rules* published in 1999 (author: Marcus Buckingham)

that the number one reason people leave their employer is because of the relationship with their immediate supervisor. This finding ignited a focus by businesses on supervisor and management training, in the hopes of improving these important relationships. Almost two decades later, the 2007 Global Workforce Study by Towers and Perrin[2] highlighted changes in the workforce that are significant. This research suggests that employees are looking for more than good relationships with their supervisor: Employees are drawn to and more likely to stay with organizations in which the senior leadership, and the organization overall, has a good reputation. Employees also want opportunities for learning and development. In addition, I believe that employees are looking for an organizational culture that aligns with their personal values.

What is a Compelling Purpose?

Unfortunately most leadership experts don't identify their company's *raison d'être*[3] as a compelling purpose. Most leadership experts still refer to it as a vision and mission. But a compelling purpose is very different from the company's vision and mission statement. Firstly, most vision and mission statements reference the customer or end user of the products or services. Secondly, a vision and mission statement is beautifully designed and framed and usually posted on the wall and given place of prominence on websites and in corporate literature. It sometimes feels like a marketing campaign. The mission statement

---

2. www.towersperrin.com

3. *Raison d'être* is a phrase borrowed from French that means "reason for being"

focuses on what the organization endeavours to do, while the vision statement describes how the company sees itself in the future. A compelling purpose will never need to be posted on the wall, precisely because it is intrinsic to the organization and the organizational culture. I have chosen the word "compelling" for a very specific reason: People in the organization feel compelled to engage, to follow, with a true connection to the purpose. It is at the core of the organization, valued above everything else.

I will begin by looking at the compelling purpose of an individual. This will help to define the term "compelling purpose" and to explain its importance. Then, I will examine a couple of organizations that have followed a compelling purpose since inception, as well as a few that are trying to define and live a purpose that they have discovered along the way.

Ryan Hreljac is a young man who discovered his clear and compelling purpose at an early age. He grew up in Kemptville, Ontario (near Ottawa), an average young boy with brown curly hair and an appetite for computer games, hockey and football. When he was in Grade 1 and six years old, his teacher was educating the students about Africa and what it was like to live there. She explained that sometimes children die because they do not have clean drinking water. She explained that if there were wells to access clean drinking water it would be a great help.

Ryan's heart was captured right in that moment. He could not believe that there were children in the world living without clean drinking water. Ryan began to do extra chores as a way of raising money. He got his brother and some of the neighbourhood children involved. He did all kinds of extra chores—raking leaves, doing dishes, vacuuming the house and, within a short period of time, he raised $70. Then, he and his mom contacted an organization that built wells in Africa. Unfortunately, they discovered that $70 would purchase a hand-pump but it was $2000 to drill a well. While most kids would probably have lost interest, Ryan didn't. He was compelled to raise the money to build a well in Africa. He simply said, "I'll do more chores and raise the $2,000." When his friends and the neighbourhood children lost interest in doing extra chores and raising the money, he did not. In short order, Ryan had raised enough money to drill his first well in Africa. Now, *that* is a compelling purpose.

A compelling purpose doesn't fade away. It exists at the core of the person. Ryan didn't raise money and build wells to become famous or be recognized; he did it because he was compelled to. He just had to.

Now 19 years old, Ryan is still very involved in building wells for clean drinking water. As I write this book, Ryan has been responsible for building more than 518 wells that provide clean drinking water to over 640,000 people in 16 countries. He is still compelled to help. He works hard to spread the message of the importance of clean drinking water for people around the world (www.ryanswell.ca).

Do You Know Your Compelling Purpose?

The size and impact of the compelling purpose is not what is important. What matters is that you identify it, embrace it and live it. Ryan is an example of a person who, early on, identified his personal compelling purpose. It was something—a reason for being, for doing—that grabbed him. I often wonder whether he picked the compelling purpose or whether the purpose picked him, but regardless of how they came together, they did. It was the union between a person and the cause that had the momentum to produce significant change in our world. An individual's compelling purpose does not have to be as grand as Ryan's. Often a compelling purpose is simple and meaningful to the person without being so for an entire community. Ryan's compelling purpose is significant and it reminds us of the importance and impact that one person can have on the world. While each of us impacts our world simply by living our life, some of us have a greater impact than others. So, it is with organizations.

Do You Know Your Organization's Compelling Purpose?

Some organizations are created out of a core purpose—a purpose that was meaningful to the founder. The challenge with an organizational purpose is ensuring that it has longevity and that it can be meaningful to others. Unlike Ryan, organizational leaders want—and need—others to work with them.

A good example is Patagonia, founded by Yvon Chouinard, who has written *Let My People Go Surfing: The education of a reluctant businessman.*[4] As I read the book, I could feel the enormous love Yvon had for mountain climbing, his passion for fishing and the outdoors. He could have been described as a hobo when he was a young man due to his love for living outdoors and experiencing the mountains and coastlines. Pictures in the

---

4. Yvon Chouinard. *Let My People Go Surfing: The education of a reluctant businessman.* 2005. Penguin. pp. 17-19, 56.

book show him sleeping under a tarp in a sleeping bag, on the side of a mountain, without even a tent. He looks content and happy, as if he were truly living his purpose. He writes:

> In Yosemite we called ourselves the Valley Cong. We hid out from the rangers in nooks and crannies behind Camp 4 when we overstayed the two-week camping limit. We took special pride in the fact that climbing rocks and ice-falls had no economic value in society. We were rebels from the consumer culture. Politicians and businessmen were "greaseballs", and corporations were the source of all evil. The natural world was our home. (p. 18)

Reading the book, I could feel Yvon's sense of connection with nature, the environment and a world larger than himself. I would describe Yvon's exploring and living with the natural environment as a compelling purpose. Yvon writes: "The natural world was our home … We were like a wild species living on the edge of an ecosystem—adaptable, resilient and tough" (p. 18).

He describes his displeasure with some of the equipment used for mountain climbing:

> In 1957 I went to a junkyard and bought a used coal-fired forge, a 138-pound anvil, and some tongs and hammers and started teaching myself blacksmithing. I wanted to make my own climbing hardware, since we were starting to climb the big walls in Yosemite on multiday ascents that required hundreds of piton placements. The soft iron pitons imported from Europe were meant to be placed once and left in the rock …

I made my first pitons from an old chrome-molybdenum steel blade from a harvester, and TM Herbert and I used them on early ascents of the Lost Arrrow Chimney and the North Face of Sentinel Rock in Yosemite. These stiffer and stronger pitons were ideal for driving into the often incipient cracks in Yosemite and could be taken out and used over and over again. (pp. 15-17)

Most of my tools were portable, so I would load up my car and travel up and down the California coast from Big Sur to San Diego. I would surf, then haul my anvil down to the beach and cut out angle pitons with a cold chisel and hammer before moving on to another surfing beach ...

For the next few years I worked on my equipment in the winter months, spent April to July on the walls of Yosemite, headed out of the heat of summer for the high mountains of Wyoming, Canada, and the Alps and then back to Yosemite in the fall until the snow fell in November. During these times I supported myself selling the equipment from the back of my car. The profits were slim ...(p. 18)

[In 1964] I put out my first catalog, a one-page mimeographed list of items and prices with a blunt disclaimer on the bottom saying not to expect fast delivery during the months of May to November. (p. 21)

This was the beginning of the Chouinard Equipment Company and the future Patagonia (named after the Patagonia Mountains in Chile), now a large and successful outdoor sports equipment and clothing company.

But what really happened here? I believe an individual's

passion for the outdoors and the environment morphed into a business enterprise, a company. My sense is that people who shared this love were drawn to the company that served the outdoor life, whose founder (Yvon) participated in outdoor sports, and whose work honoured nature and the environment: "We continued to hire friends, as we needed more help" (p. 25). I believe the company grew because the people attracted to the company were drawn to its compelling purpose. Is it possible the company organically attracted men and women who honoured and cared for the outdoors, who lived like this naturally, who chose this as a philosophy rather than as a business model? This way of living and working was simply the right thing to do.

It seemed to me as I read the book that Patagonia became one large family with friends and relatives being hired and babies being born and introduced into the work environment shortly after birth. Yvon's wife Malinda is quoted on her views of child care:

> It didn't start out by careful design. Even though my minor was in home economics, I was one of the few to graduate completely devoid of any classes in preschool training. The real root of our day care center was that the Frosts brought their babies to work, so we did too. As we hired new employees they followed suit. Baby beds were draped over computer monitors, to the horror of those who understood computers, but it wasn't until the arrival of one baby, born a screamer, that we realized the havoc the babies created in the workplace. The baby's mother took to sitting in the car outside with the colicky infant, and we all felt guilty.

The idea of devoting either cash or space, both in short supply, to infants was debated for two more years. We had no idea how to start a day care center, but several parents pushed ahead with the idea. Long after it was opened, we learned that it was a radical idea, one fraught with laws and hysterical parents. (p. 56)

It seems to me that, to this day, Patagonia remains driven by its compelling purpose, not only to make quality outerwear but, as one of their primary focuses, to build sustainability and renewability into all of their practices. When you visit their website you will quickly see all of their environmental initiatives: to choose vendors using strict criteria, to ensure that their environmental impact is minimal and to work towards renewability and sustainability. They personally and financially support environmental causes.

Patagonia employees are personally involved in the initiatives. One example of their passion is helping to create a new national park. In 2004, former Patagonia CEO, Kristine Tompkins, bought 173,000 acres through the nonprofit foundation, Conservacion Patagonica.[5] The goal is to permanently protect the land—or estancia as they say in Spanish—for many years to come while restoring it to its natural state.

---

5. Created in 2000, Conservacion Patagonica has already placed 460,000 acres of critical Patagonian habitat into permanent protection. We've successfully created one Argentine national park, and are in the process of creating a second in Chile. We are results-oriented and seek conservation projects on a grand-scale, where strategy and actions are driven by the desire to achieve the highest level of conservation possible. (http://www.conservacionpatagonica.org/)

I believe these are people living their compelling purpose who know they have a connection to the larger community. They know that their impact is bigger than just creating outdoor equipment and clothing. They know their impact brings value much greater than profits, and their philosophy encourages team collaboration and unity. They are drawn to and committed to the company's compelling purpose by their love of the outdoors and the natural environment.

The people who work at Patagonia appear to be driven by a compelling purpose that they live and breathe: It is their very reason for being in business. Do they make money? Absolutely. Do they make quality and in-demand clothing lines and outdoor equipment? Absolutely. Do they do this in a way that is congruent with their compelling purpose? Absolutely. They work hard to keep the outdoor environment healthy and pristine, to ensure there is a place for mountain climbing and surfing and any other outdoor sport in which people want to participate.

While an excellent example of a company founded on a compelling purpose, Patagonia is not unique. There are many examples of companies that have a compelling purpose or who are, in the process of being in business, finding their purpose.

Another example of a company with a compelling purpose is Mary Kay, the cosmetics company, which was started by Mary Kay Ash. Her compelling purpose was to provide a way for women of the southern U.S. to make a living and become financially independent: "To provide women with an unparalleled opportunity for financial independence, career and personal fulfillment." This was always the compelling purpose behind Mary Kay Cosmetics. Mary Kay Ash also believed in living and working by the Golden Rule[6] and putting families ahead of business. What type of people would Mary Kay Cosmetics attract? Women who wanted to be financially independent, women who wanted to be free from the constraints of relying on others. As long as Mary Kay Cosmetics stayed true to its compelling purpose by providing these opportunities in a real and meaningful way, the company would attract the right people who were drawn to its purpose.

In conversation with a Mountain Equipment Coop (MEC) employee, I learned that this Canadian cooperative is focused on member services and selling products that meet the demands of the outdoor enthusiast. The passion that was reflected by this employee was significant. Their positive language and ability to describe in detail the value that MEC provides its members was inspiring. One statement went something like this: "We are a real family ... on days off, you will often find co-workers sharing in outdoor adventures and activities. We have a common interest that shows in everything we do, whether it is at work or hiking on a day off."

I have always been fascinated by Southwest Airlines and the company's ability to engage over 32,000 employees across its numerous locations. What is the magic that sets them apart from other airlines? I believe it has been a focus on the human

---

6. ... in 1963 ... Mary Kay Ash enlisted the help of her 20-year-old son, Richard, and created Beauty by Mary Kay. It was a first—a company dedicated to making life more beautiful for women. It was founded not on the competitive rule but on the Golden Rule—on praising people to success—and on the principle of placing faith first, family second and career third. It was a company, as Mary Kay Ash often said, "with heart." (http://www.marykay.com/company/companyfounder/default.aspx)

beings within the organization and the company's ability to tap into the unique talents of each person. They value the employee above the customer, knowing intuitively that if they look after their employees, their employees will look after their customers. They do not just say this or post it on the wall in a mission statement, they live it every day. They put into practice what they believe. Their employee-focused approach has rewarded them with amazing productivity and significant customer loyalty. They live a philosophy that fundamentally seeks to ensure the first customer is the employee and the second customer is the guest.[7] It could be said that their compelling purpose is to hire altruistic individuals who are drawn to providing exceptional service to others and then to provide those individuals with a place where they can do what they do best every day. What kind of person would be attracted to this organization?

A Compelling Purpose does not Fade or Waiver

A key factor with an organization's compelling purpose is that it must endure even when, in the short term, it is inconvenient or unprofitable.

The recent economic challenges have created unique issues for some organizations with highly ingrained corporate cultures. Some organizations build a culture that makes them a fun place to work. They become known for their great environment, fun approach to business and commitment to social community. They live this culture by having Fun Days, supplying food and drinks for the kitchen, and encouraging employees

---

7. "It's So Simple", Southwest Airlines company video.

to share meals together on a regular basis. They pride themselves on being known as a great place to work. However, during times of recession, organizations can experience difficult times, and often the first thing to go is the fun. No longer is there food in the refrigerator; shared meals no longer happen. Frontline employees see things change quickly and they don't necessarily understand: How can a company believe that a relaxed and fun environment is so critical one day and the next abandon this approach for a more traditional one? Employees begin to ask: "If this was so important for so long and has always been at the core of who we are, then why could we not find other places to reduce costs before removing the one thing we all believed in—the one corporate characteristic that made us unique and special as a company?" With important cultural elements removed, the senior leadership's credibility can suddenly come into question. Could senior management have made different decisions? Would staff continue to work hard and be fully engaged, even in times of change?

Often, organizations look for the low-hanging fruit (quick cuts) instead of being creative and innovative in their fiscal responsibility. The result is seen and felt throughout the organization. Some of the best companies in the world that have survived incredibly difficult times achieved their success through innovative cuts in spending across the organization, including the salaries of the leadership team. In one organization, the CEO and entire executive management team took a cut *before* they asked the staff to take a cut. No jobs were lost and the impact, although difficult, was shared amongst everyone and spoken about openly.

The compelling purpose of an organization cannot be the

flavour of the month. It must be intrinsic to who you are, intrinsic to the organization. The compelling purpose never fades. It does not die. It is the constant guide, through good times and bad, through challenges big and small.

Developing a Compelling Purpose

There is no cookie-cutter approach, no one-size-fits-all method to developing and establishing a compelling purpose, so I cannot provide you with the seven steps to a compelling purpose. Developing a compelling purpose is a process that explores what's meaningful to the employees. It is amazing to me how when we engage our employees in meaningful conversations about the future of our organizations they have clear ideas about what it should look like. When given the opportunity, employees can provide insight into what a compelling purpose would feel like to them. They have ideas about how an organization can align its values and direction through a compelling purpose that matters. We just have to ask them. It is that simple.

The examples I have provided thus far are those companies who have had a compelling purpose from inception, usually created by the founder. However, a compelling purpose can be identified well into the life of the organization by a group of stakeholders. Created in the right circumstances and with all stakeholders involved, a compelling purpose can be a rich cross-section of the beliefs, values and purpose of the organization and its members. A company can be reinvented and reinvigorated long after it was originally founded. But it takes a significant commitment to reinvent and transform an organization. You must take stock of where the company is at today in order to determine the length of time and commitment required to move it to a future state. The timeline will depend on where the organization is starting from.

There are many different ways to identify an organization's compelling purpose and direction for future consideration. Here are a few ideas. The compelling purpose can be flushed out by using cross-functional teams, focus groups and even a large organization-wide World Café.[8] These events provide stakeholders with an opportunity to articulate what they see as critical to the core of the organization. When you involve the entire community in the process you will get engagement and buy-in and, more importantly, you will have an inclusive representation of ideas. It is fundamental to create critical thinking questions around what the stakeholders believe should be at the core of the organization. You want to uncover what truly compels stakeholders. What opportunities are there to contribute to the greater community at large? What do your customers, vendors and internal employees believe is at the core, or should be at the core, of the organizational purpose? If you were to attach your name to a compelling purpose (something you could be very proud of) what would it be? Allow stakeholders to articulate in a positive way the core purpose they believe the organization should engage in. Throughout this process of exploration, the focus should be on finding commonalities in a desired purpose. The key is to have a compelling purpose that

---

8. "As a conversational process, the World Café is an innovative yet simple methodology for hosting conversations about questions that matter. These conversations link and build on each other as people move between groups, cross-pollinate ideas, and discover new insights into the questions or issues that are most important in their life, work, or community." http://www.theworldcafe.com/what.htm

will guide decision making and actions. It must be something that can be lived at all times regardless of the business environment. It cannot come and go as convenient.

Once the compelling purpose is identified, the organization is ready to reflect on its current state in order to then determine the changes required to begin aligning policy, process and organizational direction to the compelling purpose. Organizations must be willing to do some serious truth telling about who they are and what their current corporate culture is truly like. The organization must be honest with itself and be willing to hear the truth from employees and other stakeholders. As a consultant, I am amazed at how often senior leaders have a perception of where the organization is at that turns out to be very different from the perception of frontline employees and supervisors. I ask the senior leaders to speculate about what their employees say about their organization when they are not at work; what would they tell a friend about what it is like to work there? The answers do not always reflect the senior leaders' perspective! But unless the organization can be brutally honest about who it is and where it's at in the present moment, it cannot determine the starting place for change. We must be willing to step into the prickly areas of our corporate culture if we are to build an effective plan and process to take us into a new desired future state. The payoff for any pain you may experience in the process is a positive and lasting impact on your corporate culture.

In my view—and in my experience—it is not overly difficult to define the compelling purpose or to build a process and procedure to take us from the old status quo to a New World Leadership model. The real difficulty lies in defining clearly and accurately where the organization is at today. Many organizations are unwilling to explore their present true corporate culture. However, if you begin a change initiative at the wrong starting line, you will always be behind or ahead, thus making progress unclear and unstable.

During the change process it is important to align the management process (transactional) and the leadership and leading of teams (transformational). These two functions should be aligned and moving in the same direction supporting and reflecting each other. With any change initiative we need to identify where we are today, where we want to go (what needs to be changed) and the path we will take to get there.

Companies considering the journey of defining their compelling purpose well into the life of the company must remember that those that did it from inception had to make incremental decisions along the way. Each decision required consideration of whether it reflected the specific intentional choices of the company's compelling purpose. They may not have articulated it this way but this is exactly what they did. This is not difficult. This is about being committed to the purpose, being intentional and conscious in actions and behaviour, and aligning every action and decision to the purpose.

If You Build It They Will Come

Maybe you're thinking that this is too much to ask of employers. Maybe you're saying to yourself that the younger generations are selfish and focus only on what they want out of their work-life. Well, maybe, but I say we should embrace this new reality and ask ourselves, "Why is it a bad thing to want balance, appreciation and an opportunity to work for an organization that has a true compelling purpose that allows employees to contribute in a real way?" This reminds me of that old cliché, *We can't attain new results by doing the same old things.* Our willingness to move away from the traditional command-and-control approach is a critical step in engaging employees.

With the increase in recent years of Employee Assistance Programs, stress at work and generally dissatisfied employees, we need to embrace defining our compelling purpose and our evolution towards New World Leadership. New World organizations know what compels them. They are confident in this fact and are able to articulate their compelling purpose and resulting organizational culture. They can answer the question, *Why should I work for you?* People who are attracted to the compelling purpose will be attracted to the organization as employees.

What if our compelling purpose could attract the right people directly to us? What if it brought those people to us who intrinsically fit with the organizational purpose and culture? Imagine the changes we could make to our recruitment strategies! Employment candidates have more autonomy during the selection process than they have at any other time in their employment. They are in the driver's seat, so why not have a compelling purpose that you can be proud of and that will clearly allow the candidate to assess fit for themselves? We can begin to develop interview questions around the compelling purpose, allowing us to much more easily determine the fit of the potential new employee.

More and more companies are seeing a critical link between having a compelling purpose and being successful in attracting and retaining the talent and knowledge that has a direct impact on the organization's productivity and bottom-line profits. When a company takes a holistic approach to its compelling purpose it automatically aligns with attraction, retention and branding efforts. If you attract people who are compelled by your organization's purpose and culture, you are automatically providing the opportunity for them to engage meaningfully in their work. Research shows that if you engage employees in their work, you are likely to retain them over the long term. Long-term employees will be those who will feel intrinsically connected to the organization and the work of the organization. They will feel an emotional connection to the business that goes well beyond "just" delivering results. People will deliver results with passion, engagement and a genuine connection to the organization and its people, all of which contributes to the success of the organization. In fact, this increased connection and engagement can increase productivity and profitability exponentially.

Not Every Compelling Purpose is the Same

Patagonia is an example of a company that started over 40 years ago grounded in a compelling purpose that is clear, strong and real. It is focused externally through its environmental initiatives, but ultimately their compelling purpose significantly impacts the employees inside the company. Patagonia's compelling purpose also aligns with the products and services it sells. It's a direct connection.

However, some compelling purposes are not as easy to see or articulate, yet they are just as real. Take, for example, the company that has chosen to be directly involved in Habitat for

Humanity by providing funds, people and resources to build homes every year. This compelling purpose does not align with the product or services that the company provides its customers, but every year the company's staff build three to four houses as a way of giving back to the community. The company pays the employees' salaries and everyone builds together as a team. This company has decided that this activity, though not related to its paying business, is at the core of the organization's purpose.

Some might wonder how this is any different than any other "corporate social responsibility" commitment. Well, the key difference is that corporate social responsibility commitments are usually add-ons or extra-curricular activities for the employees; they are not fundamental to the very core—or compelling purpose—of the organization.

Another example of a compelling purpose that does not align directly with the company's core service or product is that of my consulting practice, Change Innovators Inc. I often say that I founded the company as an experiment: Our compelling purpose is to provide a place for people to come to work and genuinely be themselves. There are no rules, only guidelines. Each person's objective is to explore what they do best. While our work is about providing Human Resource services to our external clients, within the organization we engage consciously and intentionally in New World Leadership practices such as responsible self-management and authentic relationships. Indeed, our compelling purpose *is* to practice New World Leadership every day.

In Chapter 3, I look at how values that reflect your compelling purpose must be ingrained in every organizational decision that is made.

Chapter Three

Values

VALUES ALIGN WITH COMPELLING PURPOSE

Values must reflect the organization's compelling purpose, and
must be embedded in everything, but not articulated in the
traditional manner of a vision and mission statement.

Organizational values make up the second element of New
World Leadership; these values must align with the organization's compelling purpose. This is of critical importance.
The organization's acts, deeds and decisions must align directly
with its compelling purpose.

Your compelling purpose and your values are different from
a traditional vision and mission statement. A compelling purpose must be lived each and every day. It is not something you
are aiming for or working towards. It is not a lofty goal. It is
a way of life, a way of being, a unique approach or strategy to
business life. Therefore, you cannot pull your vision and mission statement off the wall and replace it with your compelling
purpose; the minute you take your compelling purpose and
its associated values and post them on the wall, you diminish
them.

A vision and mission statement describes a state you are trying to reach and what you are doing to get there, but a compelling purpose and congruent values reflect how you are living and working _right now_. When there is a clear compelling purpose, a natural connection exists between the organization and its constituents. This connection comes from and through the compelling purpose and values. It is as if the team members of the organization are drawn together by the common purpose and values. It just feels right.

In the 21st century, we are living in a new world where employees want and need to feel connected to something bigger. When employees commit to contributing eight hours or more a day to an organization, they want to feel a larger purpose is at hand. It is no longer just about earning a paycheque. In fact, I am not sure it ever was.

You live your values every minute of every day, whether these are personal values or organizational values. Here's what I am proposing: When the values of the individual employees align with the values of the organization and the organizational values are aligned and congruent with the organization's compelling purpose, they can be strong and ingrained. The values of the organization that align with the compelling purpose direct our decision-making and guide us in all things. As an organization changes and evolves, the values must stay constant throughout the decision-making process, actions and reflections. If the compelling purpose is clear and the values are congruent, then regardless of organizational change, we stay true to our purpose. It is this true consistency and steadfast commitment to the purpose and values that retain the talent all organizations seek. Through good times and bad, the values are reflected in all decisions and actions. It is this strong values-based alignment and focus that breeds loyalty, commitment, high morale and additional effort to support success.

The Towers and Perrin 2007 Global Workforce study[9] found that the reputation of the organization and of senior leadership was an important factor in attraction, retention and engagement of employees. This is a significant signal of the changing needs and wants of individuals and businesses in our society. Today's employees are discerning and want to be associated with organizations that do more and mean more than bottom-line profits. This seems to indicate that the alignment between compelling purpose, values, action and decision-making is critical to organizational reputation and, hence, to attracting the right employees, for the right reasons, and retaining those employees for extended periods. Today's workers want this clear alignment not as a *"nice to have"*, but as an obvious connection between what the organization believes, says and does.

Never before has corporate reputation been as important as it is in today's business environment. A positive reputation takes years to develop but can be destroyed quickly. The alignment between what we say and what we do is the key factor in building a positive reputation. The degree to which an organization's values align with its compelling purpose is critical.

It is during times of recession and downturns in economic prosperity that an organization's compelling purpose and deep-rooted values are truly tested. Does the organization stay true to its values? Does alignment continue, even when times are tough? If the answer is *yes*, this is the sign of a healthy

---

9. www.towersperrin.com

organization that has the ability to survive even the toughest challenges. This is when loyalty is created, nurtured and sustained.

When like-minded people are drawn to the compelling purpose and values of an organization, they are far more likely to align with its corporate strategy, goals and outcomes. When this alignment is in place, employees will engage in a way that is significant, that is so powerful it can move an organization from good to great with little effort.

Employee Engagement

I define "employee engagement" like this: When employees have a heightened connection emotionally, spiritually and intellectually to their organization, its leaders and their co-workers, they put additional effort into their work that is well beyond what is required to merely do a good job. This becomes self-perpetuating: Employees who have a heightened connection to their organization, supervisor and co-workers are more likely to be engaged and will, therefore, put additional effort into their work. I believe this heightened connection is created through fully aligned and lived corporate values.

We see this in organizations where employees are connected to a common compelling purpose and congruent values. It is the heightened connection that produces discretionary effort, improved retention rates and, of course, increased productivity and overall improved morale.

Connecting Purpose, Values and Leadership

Two things are critical: to build internal leadership programs that are focused on the compelling purpose of the organization and its deep-rooted values; and to choose the organization's internal leaders very carefully.

Firstly, when considering the development of an internal leadership program it is critical to ensure that the compelling purpose and values are woven through all elements. Consistency with the values, decision-making, relationship building and communication is integral to the credibility of the training. Building a common language that reflects who you are as an organization is important to ensuring that your high potential leaders are all getting the same message.

Secondly, you must choose the right leaders—those who demonstrate the highest level of commitment to the purpose and values of the organization. These are the individuals you want leading your organization, because they bring with them an innate and intuitive understanding of your organization and its purpose. Of course, you need to continue to look for people who have the basic competencies and technical capabilities for the job, but it is important that individuals who lead the organization genuinely and sincerely understand why the organization is in business. My recent research indicates that employees want to see organizations promote individuals who have the right competencies and, more importantly, have a clear fit with the organizational values and purpose.

The problem with traditional recruitment strategies is that organizations tend to recruit to the competencies of the job only; then, when they try to recruit to the fit of the organization, they often fail. This is not because it is hard to assess fit or because the candidates don't care about fit; it is usually because the organization itself doesn't know its compelling purpose and does not feel the intrinsic values. It is difficult to assess something in others that we don't feel ourselves.

Values that align directly with the compelling purpose of the organization and that are woven into the internal leadership program allow internal leaders to go out and run the business in alignment with the compelling purpose and values. When values are deeply rooted and lived within all practices, leaders can quickly see the connection to purpose that is greater than just the bottom line. Employees are more likely to stay and be engaged when they can see that the compelling purpose and the values at the core of the organization are being lived every day.

The compelling purpose and the important values that are connected to it must be lasting and ingrained in everything the company does. Many companies find it easy to live their values when times are good, when the economy is strong and revenues are high. But when the economy is poor or times are tough, often the first thing affected is what drew employees to the workplace in the first place. The corporate values can be seen as optional (as "nice to have"), so when things get tough they are the first to go. But when this happens, the company's and the leaders' credibility is immediately at stake. Trust disappears and people feel mislead. Talented people look elsewhere for employment. I have watched reputable companies with strong learning and development cultures slash training budgets the moment economic times are difficult. Staff who joined the organization because of this learning culture quickly become disillusioned and look for new opportunity.

Difficult times will always bring change. What matters is how decisions about change are made and how change is implemented in an organization. A compelling purpose is a way of life, so when times are tough and change is necessary, the organization's values must remain at the heart of all decisions. When tough decisions are made in alignment with the compelling purpose and values of the organization, they will be understood and accepted by everyone in the organization.

The compelling purpose and values attract the right talent to your organization, but it is other elements of New World Leadership that will help retain that talent. In Chapter 4, I discuss communication strategies of New World Leaders.

Chapter Four

Conscious and Intentional

Conscious and Intentional

Compelling
Purpose

Values

PRESENCE

Maybe more than ever these days, you need to stop reloading, to clear your mind and to be consciously aware of dialect, tone, words and body language. Only this consciousness can ensure full, clear communication. You cannot connect to people if you don't genuinely hear them.

The Intentional Leader

Leadership is a choice. We accept the position of supervisor or manager or vice president. It should be a *conscious* choice. The question is: Do most of us truly make a conscious and intentional decision when we choose leadership? If we choose not to decide, we have still made a choice. Individuals must be very intentional in their decision to be a leader. It is crucial to understand the heavy responsibility that leadership requires. Today's business environment requires that leaders accept this responsibility willingly and freely, and that they understand it is a choice. It is not an honour or a special position with the organization. It is simply a significant responsibility. Many leadership programs require the leader to restate and reconfirm their commitment annually. While completing my research on the leadership factors that impact employee engagement one participant said that during the annual leadership review in their organization each manager must pick one of the following statements:

- I commit to the leadership role.

- I recommit to my role in leadership.

- I do not wish to be a leader and will step back and put my employees out of their misery.

While this may not be ideal for encouraging safe exploration of the leadership commitment, it certainly shows the organization's determination to understand whether or not leaders are making a conscious choice to assume the responsibility of leading others.

Challenging our leaders to reflect on the significant responsibility to engage and lead team members is critical. When developing our leadership programs, we must make this responsibility and commitment clear and it must be a key focus of the program development strategy.

Faster than the Speed of Light

There is much discussion these days about people's ability to multi-task, but I believe that both the term and the definition are somewhat misleading. How many people do you know who can truly and honestly have two conversations at exactly the same time? It sometimes appears that the younger generation is far more capable than older people of engaging with multiple media sources simultaneously. I have watched young employees type an email, answer the phone and read their Facebook accounts all at the same time. But are they really doing all of these tasks simultaneously or do they have to stop, redirect their brain momentarily and then return to the previous activity? The Information Age has impeded our ability to be conscious in the moment. Or has it?

Researchers are studying the impact of our fast-paced computer age on the brain to see how it is changing over time. Interestingly, the first generation of computer babies has now entered the workforce. This is the first generation born when personal computers and the World Wide Web (www) were household items. Often referred to as Digital Natives, this first generation of the digital age is now part of our workplace. A November 2008 *Macleans* magazine article[10], "Dumbed Down: The troubling science of how technology is rewiring kids' brains", highlighted the unprecedented rate of change and the significant impact it is having on the human brain. A renowned neuroscientist, Dr. Gary Small from the University of California, described how this rate of change is creating a "brain gap" between young and old; no generation in history has seen such fast-paced change or been affected by it as quickly and dramatically as the Digital Natives have. Consider that this new generation can sit on the couch, watch TV, listen to the iPod with one ear bud, play their DS GameBoy and flip through a magazine all at the same time. Then, when they get their first job, we ask them to sit at one workstation and complete repetitive tasks for a full workday. I can't imagine the frustration that young people feel entering our old still-industrial-styled workplaces.

---

10. http://www2.macleans.ca/2008/11/07/dumbed-down/

This research suggests that the brain is, in fact, re-wiring itself. Parts of the brain are under developing, while other parts are hyper sensitive. For example, the area in the brain that processes information appears to be expanding and becoming hyper sensitive. Although this research is fascinating, I believe that the reality for most of us is that we are *not* wired to do two or three things at the same time—at least not yet. I believe that the ability to multi-task effectively with any real depth or meaning is a fallacy. What multi-tasking is really about is us redirecting ourselves from task 1 to task 2 and, in so doing, not being present in the moment to task 1. We hear only part of a conversation and we absorb only a portion of the email.

Is Workload the Enemy?

Multi-tasking is a defense mechanism in the 21st century workplace. One of the greatest risks our organizations are facing is the workload we require our employees to handle. Many organizations today refuse to look at the real impact of excessive workload and unrealistic organizational expectations. These organizations do not gain productivity or competitive advantage, nor do they get full use of their employees' creative and innovative skill set. What they get instead is employees overwhelmed by excessive volumes of information that they process poorly and evaluate only superficially; reflection and percolation are sacrificed. Organizations are exposed to absenteeism and increased EAP costs due to employees' stress and depression.

How many people do you know who take work home on the weekends, talk about their excessive workloads, describe jobs that have enough work for 14-hour days but only eight hours of resources. Unfortunately, some organizations see their human capital as machines capable of increasing production beyond reasonable limits. We engineer equipment so that we get maximum production with a pre-determined standard of quality—and often, through new technology, we can make adjustments to the equipment to increase the output. However, this mechanized approach cannot be applied to employees effectively. Limits exist for human beings and, when we don't acknowledge this, we put our team at risk. Some organizations are conducting resiliency workshops in an effort to provide employees with new strategies to take on more. In one organization, an employee described attending a mandatory resiliency workshop that was clearly intended to give employees strategies for managing additional stress and workload. You can imagine the reaction from staff already under-performing due to fatigue and stress! These are not incompetent employees, nor are they uncommitted. They are simply tired of going home every day feeling that they are still behind, continually unable to get caught up.

Many of my clients battle this issue all of the time: Executives send emails and voice messages to senior managers on a Saturday at 11:00pm. Senior managers receive that email over their Blackberry on Sunday morning and feel that they must respond, so they forward and copy the email to the next level manager for immediate Monday morning action. In one of my research focus groups, one manager said, "If I don't respond to my emails over the weekend and work at least four hours on Sunday afternoon, I am so far behind by Monday morning, arriving to more than 40 to 60 emails, I won't get caught up all week."

New World Leaders recognize that overloading employees with significantly more work than can be done in the allotted time is not the way to increase productivity. New World Leaders know that to increase productivity we must genuinely engage people, provide them with time for creativity and reflection, and encourage healthy debate and discussion while providing manageable workloads.

Establishing and maintaining realistic workloads is absolutely necessary for increased engagement and productivity; in fact, many new employees will simply refuse to contribute more than 40 hours per week. Baby Boomers may think this is the sign of a poor work ethic—laziness or just self-centeredness—but the reality is that younger workers want balance, connection and conscious communication that brings value and meaning to the time and effort they put in at work. They are not interested in getting on the corporate hamster wheel and running at break-neck speed. They want to contribute in a real way, having manageable workloads and by establishing genuine connections through authentic relationships and conscious dialogue.

Go Slow to Go Fast

The old mechanistic organizations rely on hierarchy, rules, policy and procedures. They focus on structure: They "command and control". They often focus on working *in* the business and not *on* the business. New World Leadership requires that leaders be reflective, intentional and strategic with the objective of *going slow to go fast*. Willingness to bring senior leaders, managers and all levels of the organization together to debate, reflect on and discuss issues will allow organizations of the future to evolve within a constantly changing business environment.

The current practice of inundating team members with excessive workloads means that they have no time for reflection, creative thought or debate, no time to gather to brainstorm on issues. I believe this is a huge mistake. Gathering for the annual 2-day strategic session is not the solution. Being conscious and present, going slow to go fast means creating an environment in which individuals and teams gather regularly to share, reflect and debate central issues that impact the organization. This is completely different than the structured mechanistic meeting with a long agenda of decision-making and timelines attached to each item. New World Leadership encourages a free flow of information and idea sharing that nurtures creativity and innovation. I am not suggesting that we throw out our agendas and structured meetings but I am suggesting that we need to consider the value of communication and information flow for the purpose of envisioning a future state, identifying new opportunities and reflecting on what we should let go of. Free flow of information is a powerful tool for both leaders and front-line staff.

We need to consider slowing down and providing opportunities to reflect, debate and share ideas. This is the beginning of creating an environment that is ready for new opportunities and change, as it allows organizations to be able to adjust and adapt quickly and *intentionally* in both action and position. This process is discussed further in Chapter 9, Systems Thinking and Change.

Diligent Inquiry

Intentional leadership includes a coaching approach that focuses on diligent inquiry. If we are to truly understand our organizations and those who work within them, we need to learn to step back and ask questions—then listen to the answers. Diligent inquiry is about wanting to know, to understand. It's about active listening and genuine curiosity. Opportunities abound when we use this skill.

New World Leaders understand the immense power that comes from understanding the true nature of the issues within our organizations and teams. Asking questions with genuine curiosity has huge value. For example: An employee is continually asking you questions to which she should already know the answers. Why would you give her the answer every time she asks? Yes, it is faster and easier for you, but if we want to facilitate the development of our team members, we must take the time to ask the right questions—every time. We must allow our employees to answer the questions for themselves. The more we ask questions and encourage our employees to find the answers within themselves and from their own experience within the organization, the more likely they are to seek answers themselves in the future.

If we want to seek the truth about a situation, the only way to really find it is to ask questions and more questions, drilling down to the real issue. How often do we ask superficial questions that get only to the symptom of a problem instead of asking questions that drill to the core of the real issue? Team members have the answers. The problem is that traditional leaders forget to ask the questions, or they ask the wrong questions. Learning the skill of diligent inquiry is critical if we are to develop our team members, increase engagement and seek the truth about our organizations and the opportunities that lie within them. Be curious. Stop telling. Start asking!

The Communication of New World Leaders

Have you ever had someone come into your office, sit down in the chair across from you, begin a conversation and, partway through a sentence, answer an email on their Blackberry? The moment this happens, the person is no longer present with you.

A short while ago, a client told me how frustrated he is with the use of Blackberries in his workplace. His manager had come into his office, sat down across from him and asked for 15 minutes of his time to talk about an issue. He then proceeded to interrupt their conversation every three or four minutes to answer emails, take telephone calls and respond to text messages on his Blackberry. How is this interpreted by the person being visited? What goes on in his mind? *He doesn't really want to hear what I have to say; I was working hard and being productive and now I'm sitting waiting to get his attention again.* The manager's behaviour is considered by many people to be rude and inappropriate.

New World Leadership requires that leaders be conscious in the moment and capable of engaging in conscious dialogue. This requires a slow and reflective approach to conversation. It requires that the participants not reload, which is the term I use to describe that moment when someone is saying something to you but your brain is already planning your next statement, your counterattack, your rebuttal. It is critical—maybe more than ever these days—to be able to stop reloading, to clear your mind and be consciously aware of context, tone, words and body language. Only this consciousness can ensure full, clear communication. You cannot connect with people if you don't genuinely hear them.

One strategy I use when teaching communication and listening techniques is to take a moment for quiet relaxation and breathing. The techniques we use are simple meditation practices that help to clear the mind before engaging in an important conversation. When stakes are high and communication is crucial it is important to empty the brain, eliminate the noise and open the mind for learning. This can be done only if the leader has taken a moment to relax, remove the previous thoughts that cloud the mind and prepare to engage in meaningful dialogue and, most important, meaningful listening. This may seem excessive, but it takes only a moment and allows for more effective communication. You can focus 100% on the other person and ensure that you are truly being conscious.

New World Leaders engage in conscious and present-moment dialogue and assist others in doing the same. For New World Leaders, less is more: It is not about the *quantity* of information they consume and share, but the *quality* of the information. Leaders must eliminate their biases, remain open minded and apply the skills of active listening. Being present in the moment is a crucial skill. For leaders it is especially important to ensure that you are hearing your team members and that you know what the issues truly are. If, as a leader, you are constantly doing two or three things at once, you cannot be aware of the real issues around you: Do you know what your employees are talking about? Do you really hear the dialogues going on in your organization?

It is a fascinating dichotomy: Our new generations have a unique relationship with the technical world, enjoy multiple communication devices and have vast amounts of information at their fingertips, yet when it comes to people within the organization and their desire to contribute—they want to keep it real. They want actual conversation where they are actively included and heard. Leaders can give them this through conscious dialogue. It is a skill that must be practised—and it's worth the effort, because being present is a matter of respect. When leaders give their time to be present in the moment, to be fully conscious in their listening and dialogue, they demonstrate the utmost respect for those with whom they are engaging. It shows a respect for their time and their perspective, it demonstrates that the person is important enough to them that they will slow down and interact with them in a real way. Conscious dialogue is a must-have skill for all leaders. The good news is that it can be learned.

Leaders who manage from unconscious reaction rather than intentional action run the risk of not fully understanding the issues of their organization and its team members. Successful leaders take the time to be conscious in the present moment when communicating with team members. Yes, New World Leadership requires more time for, and commitment to, the communication process, but the results will speak for themselves. Team members will feel truly listened to and valued, and this will result in their deeper engagement and increased willingness to provide valuable information. It will also result in increased productivity as employees feel their input will actually make a difference.

We don't need to be running at break-neck speed to be highly productive. In fact, I would argue that we are more productive when we go slow to go fast, when we are conscious and intentional in everything we say and do.

The links between authentic relationships, conscious dialogue and personal development are significant. Given the fast pace and excessive workloads of today's business landscape, personal self-development is often (usually) neglected. We don't take time for transparent and open information flow. With communication happening at the speed of light, our ability to be truly present and to participate in conscious dialogue is always at risk. Authentic relationships, conscious dialogue and personal development—the three pillars of New World Leadership—are critical if we are to create organizations that are sustainable, can build internal capacity, are healthy and can meet the needs of each employee's mind, intellect and spirit.

In Chapter 5, I discuss the importance of personal development programs, and in Chapter 6, I explore how to create an environment that helps develop authentic relationships within our organizations. Both are powerful catalysts for employee engagement and increased organizational productivity, and both are key to New World Leadership.

Chapter Five

Personal Development

WORK WITH THE WHOLE PERSON

Offer both personal development initiatives and professional development programs to create an environment in which the entire person can be developed and recognized for their unique gifts.

D oes your organization encourage employees to participate in personal development opportunities and initiatives? If you do, you are demonstrating a real commitment to your employees' growth and development as people. Though many organizations have professional development plans or PDPs these programs often become just another formalized HR tool that's hard to manage and very time consuming. It begs the question, why do we have them?

Some organizations have mandatory professional development programming, because they believe that every employee should be trying to learn new skills, building more technical knowledge and preparing for the next job or promotion. Often it is the organization's way of identifying succession planning and ensuring that employees are able to acquire new skills each year. All organizations should have clear succession planning initiatives but these initiatives need to be well rounded and well thought out. Providing employees with opportunities for competency growth is certainly a worthy and important goal when the opportunity is voluntary and encouraged, not mandatory. However, it's important to remember that some valuable employees who are extremely competent actually prefer to stay in their role and not move to the next challenge. Every organization needs these employees: They provide balance and consistency and bring history and tradition to the table.

My recent research on employee engagement identified a relationship between highly engaged employees and opportunities within their company. Employees who are highly engaged are provided opportunities for change and offered the chance to make valuable contributions to their organization: Their engagement attracts the opportunities; the opportunities are given to those who are engaged. To maximize satisfaction all around, I believe our efforts should not focus on formalized programs that force employees to identify what professional development they will participate in, but rather we should focus on how the individual and organization can work together to identify the *right* challenge and opportunity for the employee. This might include formalized education or training, but not necessarily. Mechanistic organizations tend to focus on the formalized technical education of their employees; this approach is safer and more comfortable than working to understand ourselves and how we impact others within our team—that's a significant personal development undertaking! One approach is important for developing technicians and managers within our employee base, while the other is critical for developing leaders.

Professional development programs are similar to performance management programs. They often focus on identifying weaknesses and building plans to fix someone who is "broken". While this is not necessarily the intention, it is often the result or the message perceived by employees. What is the difference between a professional development plan and a personal development plan?

- *professional development plan* focuses on competencies and technical capabilities of the employee. These plans are often designed to improve the work performance of the individual. They often include training for specific technical competencies that will enhance the person's ability to perform their job.

- *personal development plan* focuses on the individual and their personal preferences. It includes the natural communication style and decision-making process, as well as the individual's preference for processing information. A personal development plan provides opportunities to stretch the personal approach and impact of the individual in a way that is unique to them. It is not based on technical competencies, but on emotional intelligence.

Personal development encouraged by New World Leaders includes an opportunity for every employee—not only the organization's internal leaders—to participate in self-development work. People must be given opportunities for personal development. This requires that individuals have an opportunity to participate in self-awareness activities. Many valuable tools can be used to accomplish this.

Preference-based profiles and assessment tools, when combined with the right training and coaching, can create powerful environments of reflection and understanding. It doesn't matter whether you use Disc, MBTI, Insights Discovery or Emotional Intelligence tools. What's important is to provide the opportunity for people to engage in self-discovery and to build self-awareness. This is the key to personal development. Once conscious self-awareness begins, the journey of self-leadership can emerge; this journey is absolutely fundamental for New World Leaders. They never stop learning about themselves, never stop stretching their interpersonal and leadership skills. It is a life-long journey of self-discovery. New World Leaders understand that you cannot lead others unless you are already leading yourself. The relationship that a person has with themselves is crucial to developing relationships with others. Intentional initiatives are the foundation of self-leadership. How can a person effectively lead others, if they are not already engaged in a journey of self-exploration and self-leadership?

Do you still think New World Leadership is impractical or a poor approach for a business enterprise? If so, I encourage you to reflect on the following questions and then consider the influence that your own experience has on your expectations of your work environment:

1. Are you a manager in a very hierarchical organization?

2. Are you in a position of authority from which you enjoy the command-and-control approach to decision making?

3. Have you been in the same leadership role for a very long time?

4. Are you accustomed to having significant power over the direction of your department?

Change requires a commitment to take risks. Change requires a leap of faith into new ways of being. And New World Leadership is a significant shift in our business life and work that requires different thinking. I often hear business leaders and HR professionals saying, "Why won't our young people stay at a job for a reasonable period of time? Why do they continually look for something better and, once they find it, they just leave? They have little or no loyalty to their employer." I believe this is the wrong focus. As business owners, leaders and HR professionals we often turn our attention to those leaving and believe it is a flaw in their personality or work ethic that they choose to leave our organization. Instead, I believe we should take time to reflect on what we are doing—or *not* doing—as an organization and individual leader to create an environment from which younger employees cannot seem to wait to escape.

Organizations will frequently provide competency training but not training that allows individuals to look at their personal preferences for communication and decision-making. Yet these assessments are a key component of improving self-understanding and understanding of others. It is through this understanding that we can begin to appreciate our differences more fully and then begin to truly appreciate and value the unique gifts that each person brings to the workplace. These development initiatives help employees to understand where conflict and disagreement come from. In turn, this understanding allows individuals to step back and look at issues from a much broader perspective, rather than remaining stuck in their own personal biases.

Many New World organizations have programs that not only provide self-assessment tools for employees but also for the spouse of an employee. These organizations recognize that healthy relationships at home, where individuals can better understand and value differences in their partner, make for healthier and happier people in the workplace.

Imposing our View or Position on Others

If you are genuinely committed to building high-performing teams that are effective, efficient and inclusive, your organization must assist employees in moving from being positional to being open-minded and accepting of differences, and to embracing diversity in all aspects of business life. The term "positional" refers to an individual's natural and personal position on issues and relationships. Reducing positional thinking and increasing open-minded approaches shifts the organizational culture from win/lose to win/win. When we can appreciate the fact that two people can disagree strongly and yet both be right, we can create high-performing environments. But when employees, departments and entire divisions are positional, there always has to be a right and a wrong, a good and a bad, a winner and a loser. If we can remove positional perspective from our organizational culture, then we can begin to create highly collaborative environments that are innovative, creative and effective. But this can only be achieved through personal development and self-awareness that evolves into team development and team awareness, and then into organizational development and organizational awareness.

The only way to build this type of environment into our organizations is to provide opportunities for employees to engage in personal self-development and self-awareness. Because only when we understand ourselves through accurate self-assessment can we can begin to understand others.

"Perception is reality." That's a phrase we're probably all familiar with, but do we really understand what it means within the context of leadership? It is a fundamental concept that everyone in the workplace must grapple with—leaders and employees alike. My perception of myself is one thing. The perception others have of me is another thing entirely. The perception I have of others may be real only to me and to no one else in that same workplace. Each of these perceptions is real and important and accurate to the person who holds it. The question is, how do we move away from these perceptions that lead us into binary (rather than holistic) relationships of win/lose, right/wrong, good/bad.

To move away from binary positions and begin to head towards holistic perspectives, leaders must challenge themselves to explore their answers to some important questions: What is my impact when I walk into a room? How am I perceived by others? When I lead a team, what environment do I create? Do I impose my views and opinions on others or do I value the views of others even when they are different from mine? Asking these questions begins the process of self-exploration and self-assessment, and it is a crucial first step to understanding our position and, thus, our possible biases.

Of course, I am not suggesting that differences and unique views should be ignored; in fact, healthy debate and conflict are the cornerstones of good decision-making. What needs to be considered is *how* we brainstorm, debate and make decisions in our organizations. Do we nurture a culture that encourages a wide variety of views within a trusting environment? Do we value and accept our unique differences in a healthy and respectful way? New World Leaders create an environment in which employees, team members and even whole departments can engage in healthy debate and discussion without feeling a sense of loss or jeopardy when a decision is made that does not necessarily line up with an individual's personal first choice. Employees must be encouraged to feel a sense of pride and worthiness in their contributions because, of course, no one is wrong—their opinion is just different. This becomes reality much more easily when the organization's compelling purpose and values are at the heart of all decision-making and actions and when individuals learn that strong positional thinking is detrimental to team cohesion.

When our career is in its early stages, we often rely heavily on our strengths. This is normal and to be expected. However, as we move through our careers and expand our reach, we must understand that it is possible to rely too heavily on our strengths—a reliance that can really hurt a manager when they move into a leadership role. Relying too heavily on one's strengths (quick decision making, for example) can create tunnel vision and foster a belief that one's own way is the only (right) way, rather than recognizing that it is merely one way to approach something. Leaders are more likely to be successful when they stretch their thinking, move into new areas of analysis and consider others' approaches and needs.

Leaders, Managers or Both

Organizations must have initiatives that help identify those individuals who are the best technicians but not necessarily the best leaders, and those who are fabulous managers but not necessarily great technicians. In mechanistic organizations, the best technicians are often promoted to be the leaders and, in many cases, they fail because of a lack of self-awareness that results in a lack of team and organizational awareness leading to team dysfunction, failure to perform and meet goals. It can create significant unrest amongst team members.

A *professional* development plan helps our technicians and our managers to improve their performance. A *personal* development plan is essential to help grow and stretch our best leaders. It is through this personal growth that leaders learn to be accepting of differences and open-minded to the ideas, thoughts and contributions of others. It is also this growing and stretching that assists leaders to trust to much greater depths. Through conscious self-awareness and self-development, leaders begin to see the true value of each member of the team. As long as a manager or supervisor has direct or indirect authority over another employee they must be involved in personal and leadership development, for it is crucial to understand that we *manage* process, but we *lead* people. Therefore, if our work entails managing process and *also* leading people (direct authority over others), we must be involved in *both* management training (transactional) and leadership development (transformational).

In my coaching practice, I regularly experience examples of leaders stretching and growing. Take Ken for example: He is an extremely successful and very talented manager. He is a technical expert in his field. He is assertive, driven to succeed and loves to be challenged. All of these fabulous qualities have created a great career for Ken. Ken has significant cognitive ability, which includes an engineering degree and MBA. He can produce large volumes of work, is always on task and always meets deadlines. He is a top performer who has received many promotions over the years. However, Ken has a tendency to seek perfection which, when combined with his strong drive to succeed, means his interpersonal relationships can sometimes be impacted negatively. He tries to manage his employees like he manages processes, when he should be leading them.

This is how it would go: Ken would delegate work to the supervisors in his department. They would leave a meeting with Ken believing they had understood the task he assigned, but shortly afterwards, Ken would get concerned that the supervisors would not do the work to the level of quality that he wanted, so he would slowly take back the work. Ken didn't even realize that he was doing this. His lack of self-awareness created significant challenges for Ken and for the people who worked with him. He would rewrite supervisors' reports, change process and procedure that supervisors had put into place, and generally rework his team's efforts every week. What was the result of this behaviour? Slowly but surely his supervisors, who were very capable of performing at an A level, were now performing at a B and C level. Why would they make the extra effort if Ken was just going to come along and redo their work? The over-arching result was that supervisors felt that Ken did not trust them to do a good job, and they started to believe their work was sub-standard. Ken's lack of self-awareness, his inability to see that there is more than one way to complete a project, combined with his positional approach, created an environment of poor performance and significant stress for everyone in the department.

As Ken developed his personal plan for self-awareness through our discussions and the use of a preference-based assessment tool, he quickly began to shift his understanding and behaviour. Ken was smart enough to know that he wanted to combine his technical expertise with a new self-awareness. He was willing to take a hard look in the mirror and build a personal self-development action plan. Through Ken's willingness to explore his personal style, he found methods of letting go and allowing his employees to execute their ideas. The changes took place over time through reading, debating and critically questioning his methods and approach. Ken stopped rewriting his employees' work and, as a result, the supervisors began to stretch and develop while Ken learned to step outside his personal preferences and position.

Ken came to see the impact of his actions on his employees and was able to adapt his personal style to ensure that his employees could do their best. Ken's change in approach made it clear to his team that their contributions were truly being valued. Ken was able to move from technician to leader and begin to build authentic relationships with his team members. Ken's vision is to be a leader who has not only exceptional technical expertise in his field, but also highly developed interpersonal and people skills.

Stepping Into Your Goo!

New World Leadership includes opportunities for high potential employees, supervisors and managers to participate in coaching. By providing employees with coaching services, organizations can assist employees in stretching themselves, increasing their self-awareness and their awareness of other people's personal preferences. Coaching allows managers and supervisors to discuss challenges and opportunities in a trusting and safe environment, which helps managers and supervisors move away from positional thinking and towards holistic thinking.

In our coaching practice at Change Innovators, we encourage clients to step into their goo. This simply refers to stepping into and working with those areas of your personality that are under developed and not necessarily your personal preference. Our reason is simple: Most leaders and managers rely heavily on their strengths and do not stretch themselves into unknown areas. In traditional organizations leaders tend to work to their strengths and do not address their opportunities. The simplest way to think about this is to consider a person who is very different from you, someone who has a completely different set of skills and personal preferences. Maybe you are quiet and reflective, analytical and detailed oriented, and prefer to be observant and cautious. And maybe someone you work with is direct, assertive and often speaks before they think but values relationships over hard facts. These differences can cause conflict in the workplace. When leaders step (even only temporarily) into their goo (that is, the perspective of others) by trying on others' preferences and actually experience what it is like to "walk in their shoes", they begin to gain an appreciation for those who are very different from themselves. They learn new communication and decision-making strategies. This is the tough work of leadership and it is often prickly for the leader but it is one of the most effective ways to stretch, adapt and truly appreciate the unique attributes of others. It is important to own your unique gifts and talents while understanding that those gifts and talents may not be true for others on your team.

When a leader not only is unaware of the needs of others but also has very low personal self-awareness, a very dysfunctional situation can be created. I experienced this in its truest form when I was coaching, separately, four executives from the same organization. The CEO had joined the organization only 13 months prior to my engagement, while the majority of the executive management team had worked together for several years. As I worked with the senior managers, I learned a few things about the organization: the CEO had hired a new executive member to join the team within the first six months of her tenure; she had hired three different consulting firms to work with her executive team because she was dissatisfied with how things were going; one senior executive had quit and one was fired by the CEO; the CEO was perceived as demanding, impatient and a perfectionist who believed her way was the only way. After six months of working with the four senior executives, I was told by one of them: "The executive team is now openly talking about how the new CEO is a bully." I was shocked, as this is very strong language for an executive to use about the company's senior leader. But it made the picture clearer for me: Here was a CEO sending her team members out for coaching and hiring consultants to help fix things, while she herself, in all likelihood, had very low self-awareness and self-reflection skills.

This pattern is repeated in organizations where a senior leader has not done the hard personal reflective work and spends significant time trying to fix others to be more like them, instead of appreciating and valuing their differences and working to utilize those differences to the company's advantage. I have also seen senior leaders hire and build an executive team of likeminded individuals for the purpose of reducing conflict, perceived efficiency and quick validation of ideas. But this approach often reduces creativity and innovation. Executive teams need to debate, discuss and challenge each other while valuing and considering the views of those who are significantly different than themselves.

Offering *personal* development initiatives alongside *professional* development programs creates an environment in which the entire person can be developed and recognized for their gifts. This includes developing the person's intellectual and technical competencies, while also identifying their communication and decision-making preferences, and understanding the impact these have on the individual and their team members.

To be a New World Leader, you must be able to step outside your comfort zone and move away from your own position, so that you can adapt to and connect with team members in a way that is authentic and effective. New World Leaders break free from feeling an insatiable need to defend their point of view. They are confident within themselves and feel equal to everyone, superior to no one. Therefore, when incorporating a New World Leadership approach into your HR philosophy and organizational culture, it is critical that opportunities are created for employees—and particularly leaders, both current and potential—to participate in self-development activities.

In Chapter 6, I discuss the importance of building authentic relationships to enhance engagement and commitment.

Chapter Six

Authentic Relationships

AUTHENTIC RELATIONSHIPS
DEVELOP ORGANICALLY

It must be safe for people to be themselves at work,

to share who they really are to the extent they want to.

Authentic relationships develop only when we are honest about who we are, what we value, how we like people to communicate with us and how we identify our strengths. Authentic relationships take caring to a deeper level within an organizational setting.

During a recent research project, we were trying to determine what the factors are that promote employee engagement, and I discovered some interesting information about authentic relationships within the workplace. Authentic relationships exist in workplaces where people feel comfortable to be themselves and the organization overall "acts flat". Everyone is themselves. Hierarchies don't get in the way. Politics are removed from decision-making. Transparency and communication are increased. And a positive, caring approach to others is taken by all.

Acting Flat

One of the most important discoveries was something I call "acting flat even when we are not." This evolved through a discussion with Tom, a participant in one of the focus groups we conducted. A young man who had been in the workforce for only a few years, Tom already knew—and could articulate—what he is looking for from his organization. He understood that his efforts contributed to the productivity and profitability of the organization. He recognized that organizations require people who make final decisions, that there will always be some level of hierarchy. He agreed that someone must take ultimate responsibility and sign the cheques. And knowing all of this, what he really wants are authentic relationships—even with senior leaders—that are transparent and honest. He wants relationships in which senior leaders treat him as if he were as important as they are, regardless of title, structure or hierarchy.

Tom wants to have real relationships with people in the organization, but this doesn't mean that he is looking for a best friend. It's not friendships he's looking for at work; he already has his circle of friends. He wants everyone to be honest, transparent and treated as equals. The people cleaning the offices at night are just as important as the marketing department. Each person plays an important role. Tom wants to work for an organization that recognizes the unique talents and contributions of each participant. Senior leaders must recognize the significant contributions of frontline employees and respect their contribution for the value it contributes to the organization.

Wow! I was blown away. Here was a 20-something young man who clearly knew what he was looking for at work, and I heard this theme over and over again in many of our conversations, focus groups and the World Café during this research initiative. Even though an organization is hierarchical in structure and decision-making, the relationships within it should operate as if it were flat—as if everyone were of equal importance. Specifically, senior leaders must act as if the organization were flat even when it's not—particularly in their interactions with others. This is what I mean by "acting flat even when the organization isn't."

Transparency

Employees throughout my research said, "Don't spin it. I can take the truth. I want to know what's going on." In fact, many people in the research study felt they had a right to complete disclosure of an organization's direction, decisions and strategic alignment. If they were going to contribute 40+ hours a week of their time to an organization, they felt they should be informed. Many organizations today still use the mechanistic approach of "need to know only", shutting most employees out of significant organizational matters. This no longer works; in fact, I am not sure it has ever worked. When organizations manage from this perspective, they are fooling only themselves. Often, the people involved in the situation know more than those trying to keep it a secret. For the organization's leaders, withholding information results in lost credibility and trust. For the employees, it leads to disengagement.

One specific example of the "need to know only" approach occurred when I had been working with an organization as an external consultant for just over two years. I had the opportunity to work with the management team on a special project and had come to know most of them quite well. A significant change was about to happen: Some key managers would leave and those remaining would have their responsibilities significantly shuffled. In the excitement of the change, two of the managers who would be leaving called me to share their news. We discussed their new opportunities and the reasons why they were leaving. I also received phone calls from the managers who would be staying; they wanted to discuss the impact of the changes and their new roles. This kind of communication is only natural; people need to express their ideas, concerns and even anxiety about change. About one week later, during an executive managers meeting, I was informed by the senior leaders of the changes and was asked not to say anything to any of the managers, as no one knew and would not know until a specific date later on. How could I tell these executive managers that I had known for more than a week—and so did the rest of the organization? It is human nature to discuss important issues with team members and colleagues and to keep each other informed. "Need to know only" is often a fallacy. People who care about others share their concerns, interests and possible impacts of change with their co-workers. The "need to know only" philosophy only serves to hurt the creditability of senior managers. One of two things happens: the staff all know and view the secrecy as juvenile and unnecessary; or the people who should know are left in the dark and when they find out they feel horribly betrayed and undervalued.

One other example I came across during my research is really hard to forget. When we were on the subject of authenticity and the importance of transparency and keeping things real, a young woman described a situation at her workplace that shocked many of us. She talked about how the managers in her organization receive annual bonuses for connecting with employees; it's one of their Key Performance Indicators (KPIs). Now, on the surface, this may not seem like a bad thing; however, sometimes the good intentions of leaders and HR departments are offset by negative ramifications that have not been properly thought through. In this organization, if managers want to receive their bonus and their annual incentives, they are required to prove that they have connected with employees in a real way. However, the corporate culture was not holistic in nature or focused on employee caring and connection. As a result, managers would go through the motions every quarter to ensure that they could prove they had connected with their team members. At the end of the quarter, managers would quickly write notes and thank you cards and mail them off or put them in people's in-baskets, as a way of thanking them and demonstrating that they had connected with them.

It wasn't long before employees figured out that managers were receiving bonuses for trying to connect with employees, and, to them, it then became nothing more than an exercise. It seems so absurd, really. Communication didn't necessarily improve and employees would sit around waiting for their cards to arrive in the mail, knowing full well that they were coming so that their manager could receive a bonus. What was created as a positive program by management became a negative experience for employees; the program lacked credibility and management was generally considered insensitive to employees' real needs.

In this example, the formalizing of manager/employee communication ruined what could have been an authentic process. Authentic relationships between individuals develop organically not through formalized programs. Authentic relationships are grounded in a culture that nurtures open, honest connections between people. People must feel it is safe to be themselves at work, to share who they really are to the extent that they want to. Managers must regularly and consistently recognize team members' true contribution when real efforts are made to adapt and connect to each other in a positive way.

Genuine Caring through a Positive Approach

People want to be honoured and cared for in a way that is real and authentic. Many examples exist of companies at which authentic relationships and deep caring for employees is valued and has helped to significantly improve the bottom line. Key factors that help create authentic relationships include the organization and its leaders seeing the good (positive attributes) in all team members and recognizing that team members want to contribute positively and have good intentions.

Many of these companies openly credit the genuine, caring relationships within their organization for their improved productivity and bottom line. Tapping into the potential of people through a positive caring approach can have significant impact in building authentic relationships. Peter Senge[11], a leading scholar on people and learning organizations, has written about Hanover Insurance (as just one example), which went from being one of the poorest industry performers to consistently being in the top 25% of their industry, as measured by

---

11. Peter Senge. *The Fifth Discipline: The Art and Practice of the Learning Organization*. 1990. Doubleday.

profit. The company attributes its exceptional performance to the commitment and engagement of its employees—features that are the direct result of the company leaders' deep caring for their employees' well-being. Their corporate philosophy evolved to include a caring for employees that rippled from the top of the organization through to the frontline. Managers and supervisors were expected to take their relationships with their employees seriously, while knowing that authenticity was crucial. Supervisors were picked based on both their industry expertise and their ability to engage and connect with their team members. Being a manager or supervisor carried an extremely important responsibility for relationship building that was real and meaningful.

Senge also writes about Kazuo Inamori, the founder and president of Kyocera[12], a successful company in Japan. When speaking to his managers about enhancing relationships and productivity, he said: "You require a new understanding of the subconscious mind, willpower and action of the heart. You must have a sincere desire to serve the world … duty as a manager starts with providing for both the managerial good and the spiritual welfare of employees."

Much research has been done on the connection between values, positive approaches and the beliefs of leaders and their impact on employee commitment, loyalty and performance. Leaders must take their responsibility for employees and their

---

12. The Kyocera corporate motto is: Respect the Divine and Love People. The management rationale is: To provide opportunities for the material and intellectual growth of all our employees, and through our joint efforts, contribute to the advancement of society and humankind. (www.global.kyocera.com/company/philosophy/)

well-being very seriously and create an environment in which authentic relationships can flourish. This is what the employee of today expects.

The impact such an approach can have is illustrated in the example of a friend of mine. Jane had worked for almost 18 years for a large distribution company that supplied the oil and gas industry, but after so many years with the same company, she felt she really wasn't going anywhere. Relationships with employees were strained most of the time and she had a sense that nobody really knew her, was interested in knowing her interests or in discovering what her passion and talents were. Jane made the bold and risky decision to leave her employer to accept a job with a competitor. She moved three provinces away and began a new life. Her new employer immediately wanted to know her, to understand what her interests were, how she would like to develop, what courses or opportunities she was looking for. They wanted to get to know Jane as a person and ensure that she had the opportunities she was looking for. The change in Jane within the first six months was remarkable. She could not believe that such an employer could exist—an employer who actually cared about the individual employee. Jane had found a place that she wanted to be. She engaged with her work and her colleagues right from the beginning and still loves it four years later, finding opportunities for personal growth, expanding her skill set and working with an employer who actually knows her and has a real and authentic relationship with her.

Being Authentic isn't Always Easy

Creating authentic relationships in the workplace is not always easy. We have been socialized over decades to use a mechanistic, left-brain approach to our relationships in the workplace. These mechanistic relationships have greatly hurt our ability to truly build an engaged workforce. We have managed this mechanistic workforce through layers of legislated process and procedure that has us calling the corporate lawyer whenever we have to deal with difficult people issues at work. And, because of this, our true people skills are under-developed.

Building authentic relationships and managing those relationships takes a little more time—or is *perceived* as taking more time, than the mechanistic approach of rules, laws and corporate policy. It is important to recognize that I am *not* saying we should not have laws or policies to help guide our conduct. The problem is when we rely so heavily on them that we avoid building authentic relationships, that when we get into a challenge we go to the rule book instead of to the person.

At Change Innovators, we dealt with a situation that left us feeling extremely proud of our approach and ability to navigate difficult situations in an authentic and caring way that aligned with our values and compelling purpose. (We can't preach New World Leadership without applying it in everything we do.) We hired a senior consultant from a large corporation. Melanie wanted a change and was looking for a new challenge. We were looking for a senior person who could take on a significant level of responsibility within the company and with our clients. However, Melanie had never worked for a consulting firm. She had always been a manager within large organizations. Consulting is a unique profession that requires a specific approach and skill set, but we were confident that Melanie would adjust. Within the first four months, however, we noticed that she was not performing at the level we thought she should be, but we considered that maybe Melanie just needed additional adjustment time. Along the way, I had had many informal conversations with her about work, happiness and fit within the company and culture. But by month six there were clear signs that Melanie was not happy. In fact, our entire team could see it and everyone started to worry about both Melanie and our clients. I decided to talk to her about fit. The conversation started as many conversations of this type do, with a casual and general discussion about work and clients. Then I plainly stated, "Melanie, it appears to me and the other team members that maybe you are really not happy here with the type of work you are doing. If that's the case, it's totally ok; I just thought we could talk about it." Melanie responded as expected and as trained in the mechanistic world: "No. What would make you think that? I am just fine; it is just taking me a little longer to adjust to consulting." I told her that everyone on the team really cared about her and that we believe each employee should love coming to work, but our sense was that she did not love to come to work. I told her that we wanted to be transparent and honest with our team members and that it was okay if her new job was not meeting her expectations. At that point Melanie decided it was okay to tell me that, in fact, it was not what she expected and she was unsure as to whether she was really interested in consulting. I asked her what we could do to make the transition easier, if she still wanted to work through the transition. And then I asked her, "Melanie, if you were looking for another job would you tell me?" She replied, "If you were going to fire me, would you tell me?" I was thrilled, because that question signaled to me that we were now going to have a real conversation about what mattered, her happiness and the company's best interests. I told her that she would know well in advance if we were concerned enough that we were considering changing our relationship. I asked her if she would like some additional time to explore the work, the company and her relationship with it. Melanie said she would, so we agreed that we would meet again in eight weeks to see how she was feeling. But just six weeks later, Melanie came to me and said, "I don't need any more time. I really don't like consulting. It's not for me." We agreed that we would need to put some timelines around our disengagement to ensure that Change Innovators could move on and that Melanie would have time to seek new employment. We agreed on eight weeks. Melanie would be free to seek new employment, even going for interviews during company time, and I would provide a reference. Risky process? Maybe, but for us it was the only way: The compelling purpose of our organization is to provide a place where employees can be themselves and reach their full potential while helping clients with their organizational performance needs. Within four weeks, Melanie had found a new job that was a great fit where she could share her skills and succeed. At Change Innovators, we were well positioned to move on, and our compelling purpose and values were honoured while ensuring authentic and real relationships were maintained. I recognize that this process would not work in a mechanistic environment, but with our holistic approach to people and our business relationships, it was the only way to manage this situation.

Who is responsible when poor hiring decisions are made? Often our response is to blame the employee: "They are not cut out for the job ... they don't have the skills we thought they had." The focus is often placed on what the incumbent lacks rather than on the hiring practices of the employer. With Melanie, at Change Innovators, we had to be brutally honest about who was really responsible for this situation. The fact is we *both* were responsible for what transpired. Melanie had made the decision to join our organization and we had made the decision to hire her. We needed to own our error, make it right in the most respectful way possible and move on with our values intact. We could have terminated Melanie's employment quickly and easily, as we had a contract with her and she was still on probation, but why would we do that? How would it benefit anyone? By the time Melanie and I had that first prickly conversation, she was very familiar with our New World Leadership environment and she would have expected nothing less from us than honesty—even though, initially, she was nervous about being honest. She had become used to our open, transparent coaching style of communication where everyone is able and willing to provide honest feedback.

When we treat people the way they want to be treated, and when we have high expectations for ourselves to be honest, transparent and authentic, we get back those same behaviours from our colleagues and employees.

Creativity and Innovation

When we look back on business and economic cycles we can see significant shifts throughout time. The industrial age of mechanistic process and procedure was replaced with knowledge-based workers who specialized in computer programming, engineering, law and high finance. When this was combined with the material desires, there was a strong need to achieve a high level of technical education so that a prosperous career could be established. The number of MBA graduates in the 80's and 90's was on the rise.

Interestingly, I believe that we are now seeing another shift. As our western world has attained a high level of material accumulation, we have discovered that it has, in fact, not made us happy. The mechanistic, industrial and knowledge-based movement towards achievement and success has not made our employees or the general population in the western world happy or, in the true sense of the word, more successful. We are looking for more. Once again we are on the move as a society, from material attainment to the more personal exploration of meaning. As a society we are in need of more intrinsic and holistic approaches to our working lives. One of the elements of this is authenticity and the ability to keep it real.

When we build authentic cultures based on intrinsic and holistic approaches, we begin to see the inter-connections between people and their natural creativity and innovation. This type of work environment encourages conceptualization, synthesizing and big picture thinking. These are sought-after skills that we all have and, yet, they have been considered not as important in the mechanistic, industrial and even knowledge-based economies. However, there is a renewed recognition of the importance of these skills in today's business environment: The only way to truly tap into the innovative and creative side of our team members is to provide an environment where it is not only safe to do so but it is encouraged, welcomed and sought after. It must become a high priority.

This is a significant shift for many older CEOs and senior leaders whose careers were founded on being evidence-based, logical and analytical thinkers. It is not that these skills are no longer valuable; it is just that if we continue to rely on these skills so heavily we will lose ground, competitive edge and, most importantly, the engagement of our workforce. This is true for the majority of the older (baby boomer) workers and also of the younger digital natives. Many older workers recognize that the escalator of business life, accumulation of wealth and material belongings does not make a person happy, especially if work is unsatisfying, not engaging and strictly extrinsic. The younger worker has witnessed firsthand the results of a society completely focused on logical thinking for the purpose of accumulation of wealth and power. Both groups want and need to find meaning in what they do, both personally and professionally. We are continuing to evolve as a species, and this includes our desire to find meaning in what we do and to seek new truth through creativity and innovations, rather than only through science and logical thinking. New World Leadership, which includes a compelling purpose and authentic relationships that are holistic interdependent and intrinsic, organically produces environments of innovation and creativity. When this environment exists, people are willing to share their entire skill set with the organization. This means that they will not only share their analytical (safe, traditional) skill set but they will share their creative, big picture, conceptual and innovative skills.

The word *authenticity* can stir up emotions and thoughts about being grounded, present and conscious in our actions. Sometimes we need a reminder, however, to *be* authentic. When I teach university classes, I often ask the students, who are usually up-and-coming managers: "If you believe, on some level, that we are all interconnected as human beings and have common intrinsic needs, and you know that *you* want to be cared for and *you* want to be in authentic, genuine relationships, what makes you think your employees want anything less?" The students look bewildered while they ponder this question. Many of them realize for the first time that their employees are not different from them, that they want to provide genuine value and to be authentic and connected in a real way—just like they do.

In Chapter 7, I discuss the importance of providing opportunities for employees to self-manage.

Chapter Seven

Responsible
Self-Management

SELF-MANAGEMENT STRENGTHENS
YOUR ORGANIZATION

Clear evidence exists that when people are given the opportunity to self-direct and co-create their work they are more apt to buy in, be accountable and take reasonable risks.

An organization that allows individuals to self-manage is one that creates employee engagement, builds appreciation for contributions, promotes creativity and innovation, and allows change agents to bubble up to the surface. As a result, responsible self-management is a powerful tool for increasing profitability and productivity.

People are given the opportunity to self-direct and co-create their work they are more apt to buy in, be accountable and take reasonable risks. If today's businesses must be innovative, creative, adaptable and flexible, then responsible self-management is required. But what does responsible self-management include?

Responsible self-management will look different in every organization and may vary according to industry and government regulations; and how widely it's implemented in any given organization will change by sector and context. However, the basics of responsible self-management do not change: Employees have input into how their work is done and are able to co-create the work itself.

Responsible self-management is not the same as giving employees a blank ticket of empowerment. In recent years, we have seen organizations implement employee empowerment strategies that stretch right across the organization. Empowerment that emerges naturally from responsible self-management is a good thing. It is not something you can give employees; it is something employees take because the environment nurtures it and they embrace it. Many individuals will choose <u>not</u> to make critical decisions about their work; they will leave that to managers. Ultimately, empowerment is only productive for the organization to the extent that employees are willing to embrace it. Employee empowerment is the natural result of a culture that encourages responsible self-management.

Any time the employer can allow an employee to make the decision, and the employee is comfortable and confident to make the decision, responsible self-management can be applied. Take flextime as a simple example: If an employee knows they must put in 7.5 hours of productive work time every day in a 5-day week and their employer does not require the work to be performed at specific times, then permitting the employee to self-manage their schedule—if the employee <u>wants</u> to self-manage their responsibilities—empowers the employee to manage their time and their work hours.

Ask yourself a simple question: Who is the best person to manage you? Most people answer: "I am!" And I agree; no one manages you better than you do yourself. I often ask my students (who tend to be managers and senior managers) this question, because I want them to reflect on why they believe they are best to manage themselves yet don't extend this same understanding to their employees. If, intuitively, we believe that all humans are connected by similar needs and wants, why wouldn't we understand that our team members also believe that they manage themselves best? But when we create organizations, and, in particular, mechanistic bureaucratic organizations, we seem to believe that everyone coming through the door requires management by someone else. In the mechanistic organization, we create layer upon layer of policies and procedures. In some organizations, the layers of rules make it impossible for them to move, adapt and be creative. I am not suggesting that large organizations can exist with no structure, policies or procedures. But I am asking, "How do we want our policies and procedures viewed and implemented throughout the organization?" Are they guidelines that help to govern our choices and directions or are they firm-and-fast rules that must be applied regardless of situation or context? Do we build boxes around our employees and our procedures to ensure enforcement or do we rely on people's self-discipline to follow the guidelines (policies/procedures) out of respect for and commitment to the company and its values?

I'm going to use my business as an example. When we do the interview and selection process in this organization, we are very clear that we do not manage people: We *manage* process. We *lead* people. The organization is structured as a self-management model. Everyone knows the expectations: How and when they accomplish their responsibilities is up to them. Nonetheless, within the first month or two, the new team member will come into my office and say, "I need to leave early on Wednesday for a personal appointment" (or something like this). I look up at them and ask, "Why are you telling me this? Are you sick? Should I be worried?" They say, "No, I just thought I should tell you where I'll be." I ask why and remind them that, in our organization, we self-manage and that I don't need to be anyone's keeper and that I am sure they can manage themselves best. Then they will often say, "I was just checking to make sure you really meant it. I wasn't sure in the interview that you really applied this practice." This is usually the last time I hear about their personal appointments.

It is a significant shift for most employees, and one that is a welcome change that provides freedom, opportunities for flexibility and a sense they are trusted and respected for their professionalism and commitment. We set the expectation with little or no effort.

I believe self-management comes naturally to most people, yet, over the last 60 years, organizations have trained team members to ask permission for just about everything. We leave nothing to chance. We underestimate the willingness of employees to do a good job and to contribute to their organization. The need to control everything and every situation that is so common in our mechanistic world is not a natural state for most people. And it is certainly not an environment that works for the youngest generation of workers.

These days, flexibility, mutual trust and respect are required elements if you want to see high performance. It is truly a special gift when you trust and let go and allow people to self-manage. What you get in return are committed, organized and highly motivated team members. People inherently feel trusted and respected when they are able to make decisions on matters that affect them. However, when others make decisions that affect them, without appropriate collaboration and input, most people experience a loss of control. I have worked with many companies where this approach is the status quo. I hear employees saying, "They changed the whole department, all of the work duties and rotations with _no_ consultation from the group." Or, "We work on a _need-to-know-only_ basis all of the time. If senior management believes that you _don't need to know_ even when it affects your job, your tasks, your work environment, you _will not know_ until the change is made." For these employees, there is a true sense of loss and disempowerment. They feel without value, without worth—as if there were no benefit to consulting them. Responsible self-management involves inclusive consultation and requires trust between peers and co-workers. The results are improved productivity and buy-in from employees.

Meaningful Work

As part of my research on employee engagement, I investigated the concepts of meaningful work and co-creation of work. I believe that meaningful work is a critical component of enhancing employee engagement within the workplace.

While increased participation and information are important, they will not necessarily, on their own, result in meaningful work for employees and, therefore, increased engagement by employees. Other components are involved. During my research, I discovered that in almost every case where employees described being highly engaged, they spoke about periods of autonomy during which they worked on projects, directed and created their work, and were given opportunities to manage the process and direction. They were also responsible for making decisions as a project team. A second key factor was that these employees were selected for their unique skill set and talents, and they were acutely aware of this. It appeared that their work was more meaningful to them because they had been recognized and chosen for their unique skill set.

When an employee works within a responsible self-management model, they are given flexibility in decision-making and autonomy in creation of their work. This naturally increases the personal meaning of that work for the employee. When work is meaningful, people have a higher level of commitment resulting in increased productivity.

The intrinsic rewards for individuals that result from meaningful work, such as personal satisfaction and strong self-efficacy, are crucial components of increased organizational success. Personal development opportunities (see Chapter 5) provide the chance for individuals to explore their own strengths and weaknesses. This self-exploration assists people in determining what brings them joy and helps them produce an environment of excitement and creativity for them. At Change Innovators, for example, where we provide little or no direction to employees, our consultants flourish and get great joy from the work they do. They collaborate with other team members to ensure the best work for our clients but they do this out of respect for the company, the client and the specialist within our group. Even those who prefer a more structured environment thrive once they appreciate the extent to which we value their unique gifts and talents and encourage their best through their co-creation of work. We have personally witnessed new employees, who are more analytical and detailed oriented and who prefer more direction, begin to thrive and self-manage once they understand that they are valued and trusted to do what is right for the client and the company. Of course we do adjust our approach to ensure that we adapt to the unique needs of the individual, but it is amazing to watch a person who starts out believing they need to run everything by someone else, slowly realize that in fact they have the answers, understand the client needs and know what to do.

Human creativity and commitment are invaluable resources in business. New World Leaders engage employees by providing an environment of responsible self-management in which employees feel free and feel safe and trusted to create or co-create their work. In turn, their work becomes meaningful to them, their engagement in their work increases and—what a surprise—performance, commitment and retention improve.

What I find most fascinating in this environment is that team members actually become more not less collaborative because they see and feel the big picture and they recognize the significance of responsible self-management. On key issues, they always consult other team members to ensure they are moving in the right direction. Responsible self-management is a great way to create high-performing teams.

Performance Management

Responsible self-management initiatives require that we re-evaluate our performance management systems. Rigid programs laden with scores and matrices and performance indicators have no place in a self-management environment. Team members must have the opportunity to evaluate their own work, to be evaluated by their leader and, in turn, to evaluate their leader. I believe that evaluation is a significant responsibility that must be shared by all team members. The opportunity for employees to participate in evaluating themselves and their manager or supervisor is critical, and it should be approached from all directions.

When team members know that evaluations will consist of constructive feedback (positive and critical) and will be articulated through conscious dialogue across the organization—flowing up and down and side to side, then we have created an open and conscious environment for feedback. Team members will welcome receiving honest and direct feedback from all employees—not just a few. This can be achieved through a 360-degree coaching model. Yes, it is a significant responsibility, but one that is, in my experience, gladly shared by all.

In this approach to performance management, evaluation is everyone's responsibility (from the senior executive to the newest employee who has just entered the organization) and it takes place frequently and consistently, not just once a year during a formal, often uncomfortable process laden with rules and procedures. The New World Leadership approach to performance management provides ongoing feedback daily, weekly, monthly—whatever is appropriate for the people and circumstances. It follows a coaching model where diligent inquiry is used to evoke thoughts and actions that help to move team members forward. In my organization, I also include a more formal quarterly process, but I keep it brief and involve the full circle of immediate stakeholders.

A 360-degree coaching model encourages all team members to provide feedback to each other in a way that is safe and trusting and comes with positive, constructive intentions. It is a process that can be learned by anyone, but to succeed fully it must be implemented within a New World Leadership culture.

New World Leadership nurtures a collaborative culture in which employees are expected to manage their work, their work schedule and their workload. Supported by a framework of responsible self-management, individuals have the flexibility, trust and respect required to make conscientious decisions. Policies and procedures that in a mechanistic organization would be rigid rules, instead are important guidelines followed willingly by everyone out of respect for the organization. Evaluation becomes an ongoing circle of constructive comment and diligent inquiry for the purpose of collective and individual growth and development.

In Chapter 8, I discuss the importance of sharing the leadership role.

Chapter Eight

Shared Leadership

Shared Leadership

Authentic Relationships

Conscious and Intentional

Compelling
Purpose

Values

Personal Development

Responsible Self-Management

LEADERSHIP MUST BE SHARED

Shared leadership approaches give future leaders the opportunity to step in and out of leadership responsibilities in order to practise and demonstrate their new skills.

Shared leadership is a concept that has been building in popularity in the not-for-profit and educational sectors for some time. The concept is very simple: individuals with a variety of perspectives, expertise and skill sets come together for a common goal with the intention of solving a situation or problem. Individuals share leadership roles based on the unique talents and gifts they bring to the team. Experts step into leadership roles, as appropriate, for the good of the entire group. This process is nonhierarchical and uses the strengths of team members appropriately.

Shared leadership is viewed as a social process that arises out of the natural relationships we build. We share leadership roles in our families, communities and volunteer work based on need at the time and under the circumstances. Shared leadership happens all the time naturally and, as such, does not depend on one person, but is based more on how people inter-connect and act together to make sense of their situation.

In the New World Leadership model, I adapt the concept of shared leadership so that organizations in any sector can apply the principles in a way that reflects a holistic and trust-ing approach that is safe for up-and-coming potential lead-ers. In this chapter, I explore shared leadership from different perspectives and describe how to implement a shared leader-ship approach from a holistic viewpoint. I begin by looking at the mechanistic approach to leadership assignments and then explore the benefits of a shared leadership approach.

Developing Leaders the Mechanistic Way

Often, supervisors and managers are frontline employees on Friday and supervisors by Monday. We take our best techni-cians, those who do the job really well as frontline employees, and we promote them into the supervisory role in hopes that their expertise in the subject matter will be enough to make them an effective leader. But this mechanistic approach rarely includes any effort by the company to prepare and mentor future leaders in advance. They are promoted suddenly after a round of internal interviews and then set loose to lead the troops. When things don't go very well, those who promoted the new manager scratch their head and wonder why.

Maybe training, education and guidelines are provided in order to help the new manager settle into their new role. But this support usually comes after the promotion not before. In one example, a senior manager promoted a woman into a management role and within two months complaints started to surface from employees. Many of the complaints were coming from long-standing employees who knew the organization and their roles very well. They were considered valuable employees. The senior leaders evaluated each situation and determined it was sour grapes from those who were passed over for the promotion from within the department. Two months later, the first harassment allegation arrived, then another and another. In each case, after an investigation, the senior management sided with the newly promoted manager but determined that more training was in order. Five years later, this manager is still in the role; there have been more than six allegations of harassment and more than three employees who have quit their job and moved on to new employers specifically because of the treatment by this manager. This is an extreme case, but it's an actual example of employees being belittled and intimidated. They eventually gave up complaining about their poor treatment, because they saw themselves as low skilled and in need of that particular job. They tolerated extreme conditions for the sake of employment security.

The senior leader who promoted this person has never been willing to admit the hiring error and take responsibility, nor has he been able to honestly and straightforwardly address the underlying issues. Instead, he continues to support this person. Clearly he feels it is easier to stay the course than to admit the error and make the proper changes. Both the hiring manager and the new manager are choosing to save face by simply forging ahead.

In another case, the hiring manager trained, educated and mentored the new manager, only to fire her six months later. In this case, it was a technical expert who was promoted from within because of her track record of contributions to the organization and expertise in the subject matter. Despite these skills, however, she found herself unemployed and cast aside within six months of what she thought would be the start of a new career for her.

Why does this happen? A mechanistic system of promotion does not allow for a humanistic and holistic approach to organizational development and succession planning. When there is unwillingness to put proper processes and systems in place and to accept responsibility for poor hiring decisions, it can result in poor decisions being made right across the board that serve neither the new manager nor the organization.

Traditionally, in the mechanistic corporate world, the expectation is that new supervisors will quickly learn the interpersonal and leadership skills required to manage and lead people, and if they don't, the hiring mistake made in the promotion strategy may or may not be accepted by those who made it. Then the organization will terminate or demote the individual or, worse, leave them in the role knowing full well that they don't have the capacity or skills for leadership. Alternatively, the organization might transfer the person to another department to negatively impact a second group, thus hurting the entire organizational culture and particularly the specific group affected.

Stepping In and Out

Why train someone *after* the promotion? Why invest learning and development dollars only once the person is in the role? This makes no sense. We wouldn't allow a person to practise medicine and then, once in the role, provide them the training and education to make them skilled at it. We wouldn't promote someone to be the controller of a large organization and then send them for bookkeeping and accounting courses. Why are people promoted into leadership roles and only then trained in inter-personal skills, self-awareness, communication and team building?

It is important to digress slightly and describe the difference between management and leadership. This has been written about and talked about for years, yet organizations still struggle to understand the important differences. We manage process and procedure but we lead people: Managing process is trans-actional, while leading people is transformational and holis-tic. Very different skill sets are required for each responsibil-ity; therefore, each requires a different approach in employee development programs.

If we agree that we often promote our best technicians and then train them for a leadership role, I would like to propose a different approach. As organizations build their internal lead-ership programs, they must incorporate an opportunity for potential new leaders to step in and out of leadership roles as their skills and interest evolve. I call this the shared leadership approach.

A shared leadership approach is built on three pillars: First, a leadership program must reflect the compelling purpose and values of the organization. Second, it must allow individuals who have been identified as high-potential future leaders to participate in the program. Third, and maybe most signifi-cantly, the program must include opportunities for poten-tial leaders to step in and out of leadership responsibilities. This approach to nurturing new leaders must be applied to all candidates fairly and from the very beginning. Potential leaders must know right up front that, as they go through the leadership training program, they will at some point, have an opportunity to step into a short-term leadership role. They must also know that within six months they will step out of that leadership role and return to their previous assignment.

At this point it is critical to briefly discuss the importance of leadership training content. Your internal leadership program must align with your core compelling purpose and the values of the organization. Every component must be linked and interconnected in a meaningful way. These interconnections are discussed further in Chapters 9.

Consider these questions: If every high potential employee in your leadership program were given an opportunity to step into a leadership role for six months knowing that they would return to their previous assignment at the end of those six months, would the opportunity feel safe for them? Would the short-term nature of the leadership commitment remove some of the concerns about the stigma of having to ask recently promoted supervisors to return to their previous assignments? The answer is yes, isn't it?

These are the advantages of a shared leadership approach. The objective is to give opportunities for leadership in a safe and trusting way, so that both parties can evaluate and observe the individual's leadership skills. Candidates in the leadership program will know that there are no guarantees and that they are candidates only. As part of the leadership program, every candidate moves in and out of leadership assignments as part of their development—it is the organizational norm (not the exception) to do so.

All employees would see that leadership in the organization is taken seriously and considered a significant responsibility that requires practise, evaluation and observation of the candidate prior to any permanent positions being awarded. The stigma of demotion and the anxiety that usually accompanies an employee promoted outside their skill set would be diminished. This approach makes it safe and provides a caring environment for people to try out their new skills, to experience the challenges of leadership and to return to their previous position with no permanent judgment or reflection on their skills or abilities. Once the individual has returned to their pre-leadership position, opportunity is provided to discuss, evaluate and seek feedback from the employees who reported to them during the trial period. These evaluations can be completed as part of the leadership program with few resources and little effort.

As an HR consultant, I've met many supervisors who have said to me: "I really wish I hadn't taken this position. I got into it and realized I didn't have the skills or interest to lead a group of people. Our organization wasn't ready to provide the training I needed and the employees suffered due to my inability." Supervisors tell me this in confidence, but they're not likely to admit their concerns and fears to their employer or their employees, so they muddle through making the best of it, knowing that they would prefer to go right back to where they were and start over again—if only they could.

But in a mechanistic organization this is not possible. The stigma associated with returning to your previous position and the unwillingness of many people to admit the mistake make it almost impossible for both parties (the employer and the new supervisor) to navigate through in a trusting and fair way. We have built organizational cultures that are contrary to holistic and humanistic approaches.

When a shared leadership approach is ingrained in a leadership program, every potential leader has the opportunity to step in temporarily and then return to their previous role. It is most effective when every potential leader returns to their previous role for a minimum of six months. Yes, it can be administratively more difficult and it requires a conscious focus on how and when to move people into these roles, but the results can be remarkably positive—and enduring. A sense of fairness and trust, an environment without negative feelings about returning to your previous position—these features allow candidates to explore, test and demonstrate their leadership skills and be honest in a transparent and authentic environment.

This holistic and humane approach shows a deep caring for the employee *and* the organization. It sends a signal to all employees that the organization wants to do it right, that they want the right people in the right positions for the right reasons. This approach demonstrates a commitment to the organization and its true compelling purpose, to its leadership team and to its employees and customers. Having the right people in the right leadership roles, all sending the same organizational message, creates a strong united culture.

Project Leadership

A second avenue for sharing leadership responsibilities is at the project level. Projects provide an ideal context within which to connect personal development with individuals' unique skills, attributes and gifts. This approach is key to the effectiveness of an organization and to providing real leadership opportunities for team members. However, to do this effectively, organizations must seek the information from employees to identify their interests and unique gifts that could align with specific projects.

I have suggested that an important influence on employee engagement is the provision of meaningful work to employees. Several definitions and characteristics of meaningful work exist (see Chapter 7), but for the purposes of project leadership it is important to align the interests of employees with work that they identify as meaningful. A variety of factors contribute to making work meaningful; one such factor is the ability of an employee to contribute in a significant way using their specific skill set. Providing opportunities for employees to contribute meaningfully is a key part of engaging a workforce. The sharing of responsibilities and leadership provides these opportunities. Allowing employees to move in and out of leadership roles based on specific project requirements has a profoundly positive impact on organizational efficiency and productivity.

Organizations have a responsibility to prepare their future leaders in advance, to set team members up for success, and to monitor, evaluate and provide candid feedback. Organizations also need to provide opportunities for high-potential candidates to practise their new skills and to move in and out of leadership roles with confidence knowing that it is not life (employment) threatening. Finally, organizations need to use the unique skills and talents of their employees to move them in and out of leadership roles within a special team or project environment where team members can find meaningful work that increases engagement and commitment.

In Chapter 9, I discuss how embracing change can bring new opportunities to your organization.

Chapter Nine

Systems Thinking and Change

Systems Thinking and Change
Shared Leadership
Authentic Relationships
Conscious and Intentional
Compelling Purpose
Values
Personal Development
Responsible Self-Management
Connection to Community

OUT OF CHANGE COMES NEW LIFE

Every organization and every individual within it has a choice:
Cling to the bank or jump on the raft and go for a ride!

Have you ever been whitewater rafting in a large raft with lots people and a guide? Or have you been on a kayak shooting the rapids by yourself? I like to use the whitewater rafting analogy when looking at systems thinking and change.

Mat Kas (his real name), an associate of mine, is a professional river guide/trip leader from the International Rescue Instructors Association and a Swiftwater Rescue Technician from Rescue 3 International. From April through October, he is based in a provincial park in British Columbia, working as a guide and kayaker. For six months every year, he lives and works alongside the river with his friends who are also instructors. They are drawn to the river and nature, and they love the ever-changing environment in which they work.

I have had numerous discussions with Mat about why he

is drawn to the river and what makes it so appealing to him. Every conversation leads down the same path: It's the constant change that he loves. The river is always changing; it is never the same. Every time Mat goes down the river on a raft or a kayak, the river has changed and the ride is different. A tree may have fallen into the river or a branch that was once in the river is now stuck to the bank. Boulders move and sand is washed away, making the river a unique experience every time it is challenged.

This reflects the nature of our universe and the nature of business organizations, and also the nature of our personal lives. All around us, everything is ever changing, constantly moving, forever challenging us.

The individual separate components of the river are constantly changing, and they are also always uniquely connected one to the other. As one part of the river changes, other components of the river are affected. When a branch falls into the river, it displaces sand. When a boulder moves, the gravel beneath it changes the river bottom. When a stone drops into the water, it moves reeds, which, in turn, displace water. The river, the boulders, the water, the sand—and the kayaks, the rafts and the people who ride them—all these elements are connected and interconnected. Mat and his whitewater rafting colleagues are an integral part of their environment. They impact the river every time they travel down it. And, while they're impacting the river, the river is impacting them.

Businesses are no different. When one part of the business changes, it impacts other areas. Sometimes we see the ripples of this effect, and sometimes we don't.

Each one of us affects the environment around us every

single day and, while we are affecting the environment, the environment is affecting us. We impact the department we work in with our decisions and our work. We also impact our departmental team members. Our department has an impact on the division, the division has an impact on the corporation, and the corporation has an impact on the larger community and the external environment. Our world is ever changing, every moment of every day of every week of every year.

The rafting instructors choose not to fight the natural changes that are constantly occurring within their environment. As Mat says, "The river has enormous power." The environment has an enormous will of its own. He talks about how paddling backwards to go slower than the river can cause your kayak to flip and put you at risk of drowning. If you try to go against the current, you will never succeed because it is too powerful. You have to move with the flow of the water; you have to let the river take your kayak where it wants to go. You cannot control the river or the speed at which your boat moves. Mat can navigate the whitewater with his paddle, to the extent the river will allow him to, but he never tries to control it. That's the beauty of his sport, he says. It is the interconnectedness between the environment and the river's many components—including the people on the river—that makes it so challenging and fulfilling.

The changes that are naturally produced by these interconnections are very similar to the changes we experience in our business lives. However, there is one significant difference: Most organizations spend a lot of time and many resources trying to control the natural changes within their environment. They put processes and procedures in place to stop change, to control every aspect of their business lives. Even when they see change coming, they often plant their feet firmly into the ground, adopt processes to minimize the impact and hold on tight in hopes that they can avoid the chaos. But why do they do this?

We can logically understand that change is all around us, so why are people and organizations so afraid of change? Why do so many cling to the bank instead of jumping on the raft and going for the ride?

I believe that human beings are naturally designed for continuous change, growth and personal evolution. Surely, none of us wants to be the same person 10 years from now that we are today? Sure, we will carry with us characteristics, gifts and talents that are unique to us and will always be part of who we are, but in 10 years we surely will have evolved and grown. Of course, there are some who prefer to remain static, who are unwilling to change or grow, but this is a significantly small percentage of the population.

Our mechanistic world has trained us and encouraged us over decades to welcome constancy and consistency, to design patterns that reflect the status quo, and to build inflexible processes and complex hierarchies that are difficult to shift.

Following the challenges of the Depression and the Second World War, this approach may have worked well, but in today's fast-paced business environment it can be the death of our organizations and our people.

If we can get each member of our team to be on the lookout for change, to be looking for opportunity around every corner, then we can build organizations that are flexible, adaptable and able to see the subtle shifts in our environment, which is made up of our community, our business, our vendors and our clients. It is this ability to see the subtle changes that allows our organizations to shift and move with the changing world. I am not suggesting that we should live in a world of constant chaos, but I do believe that we need to shift ourselves and be less afraid of change, because it is precisely change that brings new life and innovation into our organizations.

What the riverbanks and the rafts show us is that we have choices as individuals and as organizations. You can be willing to look for the raft coming down the river—to be on the lookout for change and opportunity. You can choose to jump on the raft—and ride the change. Or you can cling to the bank—and hold onto the past. However, we know what usually happens when we cling to the bank: Eventually we fall into the river and, often, there is no raft; it's long since passed us by.

It is important to acknowledge that we are all different, and many people prefer static systems and minimal change. What's important is to find effective ways to embrace change that meet each individual's unique needs. But simply resisting change for the sake of resisting change is dangerous to any organization in today's business world. I believe that we work extremely hard to manage change instead of creating environments where change is welcome and is navigated instead of managed.

When employees have the skills and confidence to be on the lookout for opportunity and change, and when they know and accept that there is interconnectedness among all of the elements of their environment, then our organizations can be flexible, adaptable and responsive to change. This approach minimizes fear and anxiety and maximizes opportunity in the face of change. This approach also encourages employees to recognize that when they make decisions and move, they have a direct impact on others. This understanding nurtures a broad view of our organizations and our world.

Employee Engagement through Change

During my research on employee engagement, a common theme emerged: Employees told me that they felt most fully engaged with their work when that work involved being part of an organizational change initiative. What this suggests to me is that many people enjoy being challenged at work and want to be given the chance to participate in change initiatives. They truly wish to contribute in a significant way.

To apply this information within your own organization, you must first identify the change agents within your employee base. Change agents are those individuals who have a heightened appetite for change. They look for challenge and opportunity around every corner. When you provide opportunities for self-development and self-evaluation, the individuals who thrive on change opportunities will rise to the surface.

The next step is to establish networks of change agents who can work on transformational teams that move your organization forward as necessary. When your organizational culture is receptive to change, you are creating significant flexibility and capacity within your business.

History has shown that people and organizations that are not afraid of change and, in fact, embrace it as an opportunity are the ones that rebound quickly after significant events and momentous change in their environment. Thomas Edison is a prime example: After a fire in his laboratory that caused significant loss, he is quoted as saying, "There is great value in disaster. All our mistakes are burned up. Thank God we can start anew."[13] After the great stock market crash of 1929, the publisher of the New York Times had a choice to make about the direction of the company. He issued a memo that said, "We must set an example of optimism. Please urge every department to go ahead as if we thought the best year in the world is ahead of us."[14] Instead of covering the crash on the front page, he chose to run the exploration of Antarctica as the lead story. The New York Times metaphorically jumped on the raft and went for the ride, allowing the changes to happen, to carry them along. On the first day, 15 advertisers cancelled their accounts, but the newspaper kept moving forward. As the years went by, the newspaper increased customer loyalty and navigated through difficult times by making subtle adjustments as the situations warranted. They went with the flow of the water and rebounded more quickly than others in their industry who made radical changes in an effort to not experience the changes in their environment.

Community Connection

Today's employees are looking for organizations that give back to the community in a significant way. Employees want their organizations to have a positive impact on the larger community, and many organizations are finding ways to do this through

---

13. Andrew Razeghi. *HOPE: How triumphant leaders create the future.* 2006. Jossey-Bass. pp. 19-20
14. Razeghi. pp. 22-23

volunteer work. In fact, many organizations are building community involvement right into their corporate culture.

Patagonia is a good example; it has a significant connection to the larger community, with a particular emphasis on the environmental community. Another organization builds two homes every year for Habitat for Humanity, because it wants to contribute to building quality homes that are affordable. This particular company has programs that assist their employees in building homes and revitalizing communities. Employees continue to draw their salary while they volunteer with Habitat; however, some employees choose not to accept their pay, donating it to Habitat instead. Now, that's an example of an organization and its employees connecting meaningfully with the larger community!

New World Leadership requires that organizations view the world as interconnected components in continuous flux. Generation X and Generation Y workers embrace change in a way that Baby Boomers have never experienced. The attitude of these younger workers perfectly captures the spirit of 21st-century thinking and demonstrates a clear understanding that out of change comes new life and new opportunity.

Chapter Ten

Be the Change

You Want to See[15]

---

15. Mahatma Gandhi. Indian political and spiritual leader (1869-1948)

The industrial, mechanistic approach to managing business that was developed in the 1930s and 40s does not meet the needs of either our knowledge-based economy or the younger generations in the workplace. In fact, it doesn't reflect 21st-century society as a whole. I believe we are on the cusp of significant change, and humanity itself is looking for new, holistic ways to be in the world. People want positive change in their business lives. Why is it that we continue to use old models and worn-out applications? We merely invent new words for old concepts. With our world changing so quickly, organizations must change with the times. People want New World Leadership within their workplaces; they want a holistic, authentic approach that keeps communication and interactions real and transparent.

Many managers and executives whose careers spanned the 1960s through to the late 80s were a product of their environment. I know through personal experience and numerous conversations with retired leaders that the mechanistic, command-and-control approach was expected from everyone. It was simply the way business was managed back then. It was the culture. But this does not mean that those leaders believed it was the right way or that it was the only way; it was just how things were done. Many of those leaders wanted to be more inclusive and collaborative but were discouraged and made to feel that it was ineffective and a waste of time. Generally, you had to follow the company line and manage the troops.

What I find so interesting is that, in fact, the natural human tendencies that most of us have—a need to contribute meaningfully, a desire to be included and appreciated for our skills and talents—these have always existed, but in decades past we didn't listen to that inner voice. We did not act upon those natural desires. Instead, we followed the managers of the day and did what was expected of us.

Today, however, employees are speaking up loud and clear and making it well known what they want and need. I don't see this as selfish or as the sign of a poor work ethic; in fact, I see it as quite the opposite. It is a cry to be given the opportunity to contribute in a genuine, meaningful way; to have the opportunity to feel that they are further along at the end of each day; and that they have contributed to something more significant than just another paycheque. If we look deep within ourselves as human beings, I believe that we are all searching for similar things regardless of which generation we belong to. We are looking for ways to contribute and bring meaning to our lives and to those around us. We are trying to bring value and to feel needed. Business must recognize that there is a natural evolution occurring that will require organizations to adjust and do things differently. The industrial, mechanistic approach does not work. It leaves people feeling robbed of meaning and undervalued as team members.

My many years of working for mechanistic organizations with their command-and-control approach left me as a manager feeling betrayed, undervalued and underdeveloped. My experience included several different organizations and a variety of positions within those organizations. I became very disillusioned with the business philosophies of the day. Eventually my desire to find a better way led me to create Change Innovators Inc. This small consulting company was in many ways an accident or, you might say, an experiment. I never intended to have employees, nor did I feel a strong need to become larger than a team of one. What I did really care about, however, was being able to work in an environment where I would be appreciated and valued and where anyone who worked with me would feel the same way, including my clients.

The company naturally grew out of my desire to see what would happen if people came together within one company, where no policies or rules existed, where no boss expected you to report to him/her, and no structure existed to speak of. What would this look and feel like, I wondered? The premise was simple. Let's see what will happen if we—by now I had hired my first employee—created an environment in which everyone would direct themselves (self-manage), would do what they did best, would co-create their own work, and would contribute fully to decisions and direction. Our focus was to identify the gifts and talents of our team members and to allow each person to find their natural fit.

Our compelling purpose is to provide every team member with a workplace into which they can bring their instinctive and authentic self, and which exists within a safe and respectful environment where each person is honoured for their unique gifts and talents. We strive to pass this philosophy on to our clients by assisting them with true and lasting change, one employee at a time. We make decisions as a group, including how to spend money and when to reframe our priorities. Each member has full access to the financials, and we discuss and debate new directions and when to leave old processes behind.

We want honest and candid feedback from each other, even when it is not easy. We don't take the easy road—ever. We look for the road less traveled and try it out. I genuinely believe that our team members manage themselves better than anyone else ever could. Out of respect for themselves and their work ethic, they consult other team members when they know it is in the best interest of the company and our clients.

I have watched the most amazing young talent work hard, learn new skills, and manage significant large accounts independently. Each member of our team practises New World Leadership and, yet, the concept, the model has never been discussed. This has not been intentional. We did not set out to create this model. We did not set out to build a holistic leadership approach. We simply have always treated each other the way we want to be treated ourselves, knowing each day that the work has to get done to meet the expectations of our clients.

I can honestly say that I have never experienced a better work ethic from any group of colleagues. They challenge me every day and don't hesitate to have the hard conversations when they need to happen. We coach each other and ourselves, and work to ensure that we pass this positive and optimistic approach on to our clients.

This style has not been without its challenges. We are not immune to the changing economic times or to poor decision-making once in a while, but we stand together and navigate the challenges together. There is no finger pointing. No punitive actions are taken. In fact, the very opposite is true: We forgive each other for our errors. We know how to jump on the raft and go for the ride. We have navigated some significant challenges together over the years, and we would not change a thing about those times. Each situation was a chance for us to reflect, to learn, to slow down and to redirect our focus.

University students often ask me, "How can I really make a difference when I work in a mechanistic, command-and-control environment? I want to practise New World Leadership, but my environment is not conducive to this approach." I always say this: Every leader has an opportunity to impact their team in some way or another. We have the choice to follow the crowd and align with the mechanistic culture or we can practise New World Leadership techniques. Every time you are given an opportunity to include your team members, to engage them in what is important to them, to provide opportunities for self-management, you are becoming a New World Leader. When you slow down and really listen, when you are conscious and intentional in your dialogue, you are being a New World Leader. When you stop complaining about the younger generation and, instead, look for the silver lining—which absolutely exists, you will find a young person willing to go the extra mile and to produce beyond your expectations.

We each have the opportunity *every day* to share the leadership role and to seek the best in each of our team members. The question is, will we? Will we stop being afraid of relinquishing control? Will we begin to trust that the person sitting beside us really wants to do a good job, wants to contribute in a genuine way and wants to be valued for their unique skill set. When in doubt, ask yourself this: Is it possible that if I feel this way, if I want to be valued and I want to contribute—is it possible that my counterparts want the very same thing?

Each of us has the opportunity *every day* to be a New World Leader.

Choose to be a New World Leader.

Today.

Leadership for a New World
Key Elements that guide our HR Philosophy

1. Identify a compelling purpose that has deep rooted meaning and that can be lived every day regardless of the changing environment (aligns with Chapter 2)

2. Align acts, deeds and decision-making to the values (aligns with Chapter 3)

3. Be conscious and in the moment when communicating; the other party deserves your focus and commitment (aligns with chapter 4)

4. Seek personal development that stretches and challenges your inner being (aligns with chapter 5)

5. Have authentic, candid relationships with team members (aligns with Chapter 6)

6. Stay true to the organization's core while exercising responsible self-management (aligns with Chapter 7)

7. Share the leadership role often and allow people to move in and out of leadership (aligns with Chapter 8)

8. Connect to the larger community while understanding your interconnectedness and impact on others (aligns with Chapter 9)

9. Know that everything changes every second of every minute of every day … don't despair. Out of chaos and change comes new life (aligns with Chapter 9)

About Yvonne Thompson

Yvonne Thompson is an Organizational Development and Performance specialist, with more than three decades of experience in Human Resources and Management. As a consultant and public speaker, Yvonne brings both her passion and perception to issues of leadership, specializing in employee engagement, teambuilding, team communication and leadership development. In 2002, she founded Change Innovators, a single-source solution for leadership, executive coaching and human resource management.

Her model of New World Leadership reflects her own experience in the world of business and outlines how engagement, satisfaction and success will naturally follow when people are encouraged to bring their authentic self into the workplace and more importantly are honored for doing so.